# AC Targeting Maths

# Foundation

Katy Pike

PASCAL
PRESS

# Contents

## Term 1


Numbers to 10 2
2D Shapes 10
Addition 14
Investigation 1 18
One to ten
Revision 20
Time 22
Subtraction 26
Mass 28
Halves 30
Capacity 32
Term 1 Revision 34


## Term 2


Number 36
Addition 40
Length 44
Take Away 48
Investigation 2 52
How old are we?
Revision 54
3D Objects 56
Time 58
Patterns 61
Position 65
Term 2 Revision 68


## Term 3


Numbers to 30 70
Area 78
2D Shapes 81
Groups 84
Investigation 3 90
Paper pets
Revision 92
Addition 94
Time 98
Half a Length 100
Data 102
Term 3 Revision 104


## Term 4


Numbers 106
Time 114
Volume and Capacity 116
Subtraction 118
Investigation 4 122
Block it up
Revision 124
Sharing 126
Mass 130
3D Objects 132
Data 134
Term 4 Revision 137

# New Edition

## Targeting Maths Australia's Favourite Maths Program

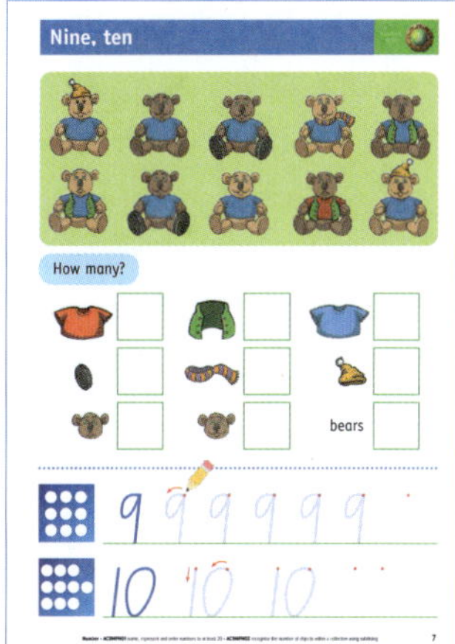
Nine, ten

How many?

bears

9 9 9 9 9 9

10 10 10

### Australian Curriculum

This NEW Edition fully aligns each student page with the new Australian Curriculum: Mathematics F-10 version 9.0. The new Australian Curriculum code and content descriptions appear on each student page.

### iPad Apps

With an app for each year, from Foundation/Kindergarten to Year 6, the Targeting Maths Apps include all the essential maths content that children need to know in an amazing app that makes learning maths fun, motivating and full of rewards. Look for it in Apple's App Store today! Made especially for the iPad and aligned to each student page in this book.

Problem solving

Ten fish

How can 10 fish be put into two fish bowls?

I can solve a problem by:

counting to 10. drawing a picture.

### Integrated Problem-solving Program

Includes an integrated problem-solving program that actively builds students' problem solving capabilities.

### In-stage Topic Alignment for Composite Classes

Great for composite classes too, the contents of each book in one stage, eg Year 1 and Year 2, match topic by topic.

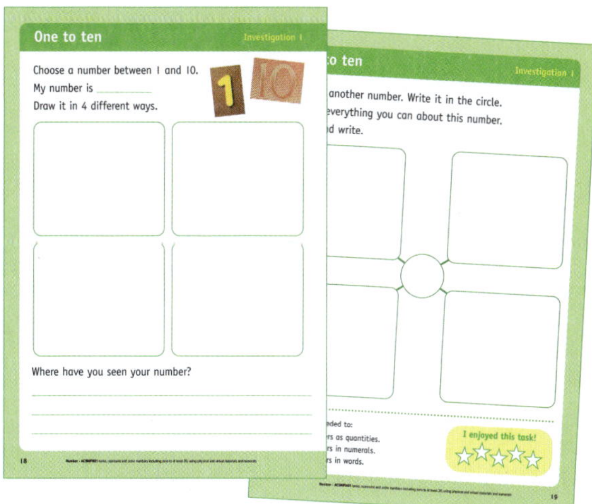
One to ten

Investigation 1

Choose a number between 1 and 10.

My number is ________

Draw it in 4 different ways.

Where have you seen your number?

### Term Investigations

Each term includes an investigation that will get students planning and working through an extended problem.

### Regular Revision

Revision pages appear both at mid term and at the end of each term to revise key concepts.

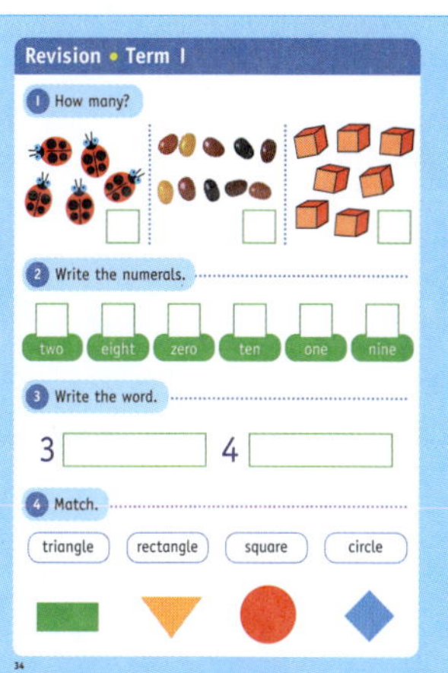
Revision • Term 1

1 How many?

2 Write the numerals.

two eight zero ten one nine

3 Write the word.

3 4

4 Match.

triangle rectangle square circle

### Hands-on Activities

Various hands-on activities are included in each term, asking students to measure and make, count and compare, using objects from around the classroom or home.

# Foundation Outcomes

| | Australian Curriculum Content Descriptions *Students learn to:* | Student pages |
|---|---|---|
| Number | **AC9MFN01** name, represent and order numbers including zero to at least 20, using physical and virtual materials and numerals | 2, 3, 4, 5, 6, 7, 8, 9, 18, 19, 36, 37, 38, 39, 53, 70, 71, 73, 74, 75, 76, 77, 106, 107, 108, 109, 110, 111, 112, 113, 136 |
| | **AC9MFN02** recognise and name the number of objects within a collection up to 5 using subitising | 2, 3, 6, 7, 48, 96, 112 |
| | **AC9MFN03** quantify and compare collections to at least 20 using counting and explain or demonstrate reasoning | 38, 39, 72, 74, 118, |
| | **AC9MFN04** partition and combine collections up to 10 using part-part-whole relationships and subitising to recognise and name the parts | 16, 17, 42, 94, 95, 119 |
| | **AC9MFN05** represent practical situations involving addition, subtraction and quantification with physical and virtual materials and use counting or subitising strategies | 14, 15, 16, 17, 26, 27, 40, 41, 43, 48, 49, 50, 51, 62, 76, 77, 94, 95, 96, 97, 118, 119, 120, 121 |
| | **AC9MFN06** represent practical situations involving equal sharing and grouping with physical and virtual materials and use counting or subitising strategies | 84, 85, 86, 87, 88, 89, 126, 127, 128, 129 |
| Algebra | **AC9MFA01** recognise, copy and continue repeating patterns represented in different ways | 12, 61, 63, 64, 82 |
| Measurement | **AC9MFM01** identify and compare attributes of objects and events, including length, capacity, mass and duration, using direct comparisons and communicating reasoning | 23, 28, 29, 32, 33, 44, 45, 46, 47, 117, 130, 131 |
| | **AC9MFM02** sequence days of the week and times of the day including morning, lunchtime, afternoon and night time, and connect them to familiar events and actions | 22, 24, 25, 58, 115 |
| Space | **AC9MFSP01** sort, name and create familiar shapes; recognise and describe familiar shapes within objects in the environment, giving reasons | 10, 11, 13, 56, 57, 81, 83, 90, 91, 102, 132, 133 |
| | **AC9MFSP02** describe the position and location of themselves and objects in relation to other people and objects within a familiar space | 65, 66, 67 |
| Statistics | **AC9MFST01** collect, sort and compare data represented by objects and images in response to given investigative questions that relate to familiar situations | 52, 102, 103, 134, 135 |

# How to Solve a Problem

**Read • Plan • Work • Check**

**Read** the problem carefully.
**Plan** what you are going to do — add, subtract, make groups or share.
**Work** Write or draw a picture to work it out. Write the answer.
**Check your answer!** Did you answer the question?

## Draw a Diagram

Draw a simple picture. Here are some pictures:

**take away**

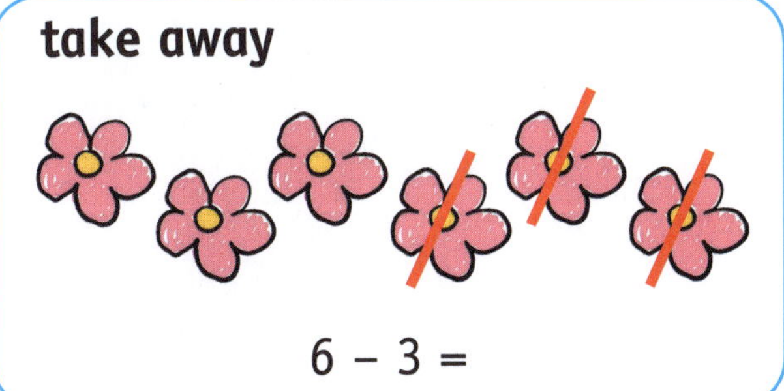

6 – 3 =

**add**

5 + 2 =

**equal groups**

2 groups of 4 =

**share**

share 4 between 2

## Looking for Patterns

A pattern can help you find the answer.

What comes next?

## Act It Out

You can use counters or blocks.
You can cut things out or
move things around.

# Dictionary

## add (+)

Two balls and one ball makes three balls.

**2 + 1 = 3**

## capacity

The amount it can hold.

The jug holds more.

## coins

## half

half a circle

half a length

## length

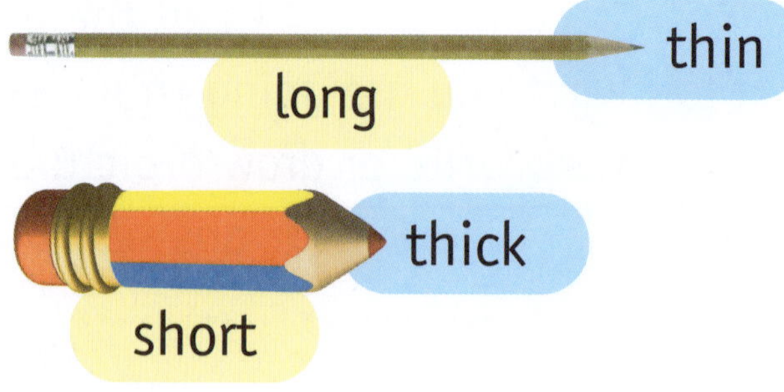


## mass

## numbers

| | | | | | |
|---|---|---|---|---|---|
| **odd** | 1 | 3 | 5 | 7 | 9 |
| **even** | 2 | 4 | 6 | 8 | 10 |

| | | |
|---|---|---|
| zero | 0 | |
| one | 1 | 1st |
| two | 2 | 2nd |
| three | 3 | 3rd |
| four | 4 | 4th |
| five | 5 | 5th |
| six | 6 | 6th |
| seven | 7 | 7th |
| eight | 8 | 8th |
| nine | 9 | 9th |
| ten | 10 | 10th |

# Dictionary

## position

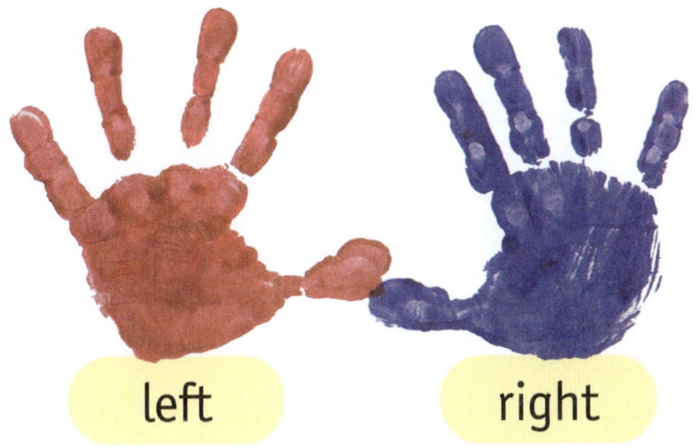

## shapes

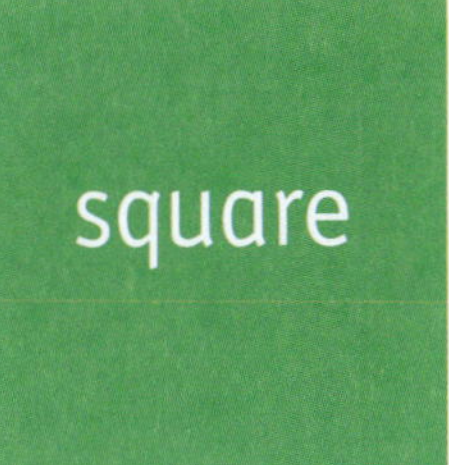

rectangle

## shapes

## take away (–)

Three cats and one walks away.

**3 – 1 = 2**

## time

**Days**
Sunday
Monday
Tuesday
Wednesday
Thursday
Friday
Saturday

3 o'clock

**Seasons**
Summer
Autumn
Winter
Spring

# One, two, three

Draw petals.

3 1 5 2 4

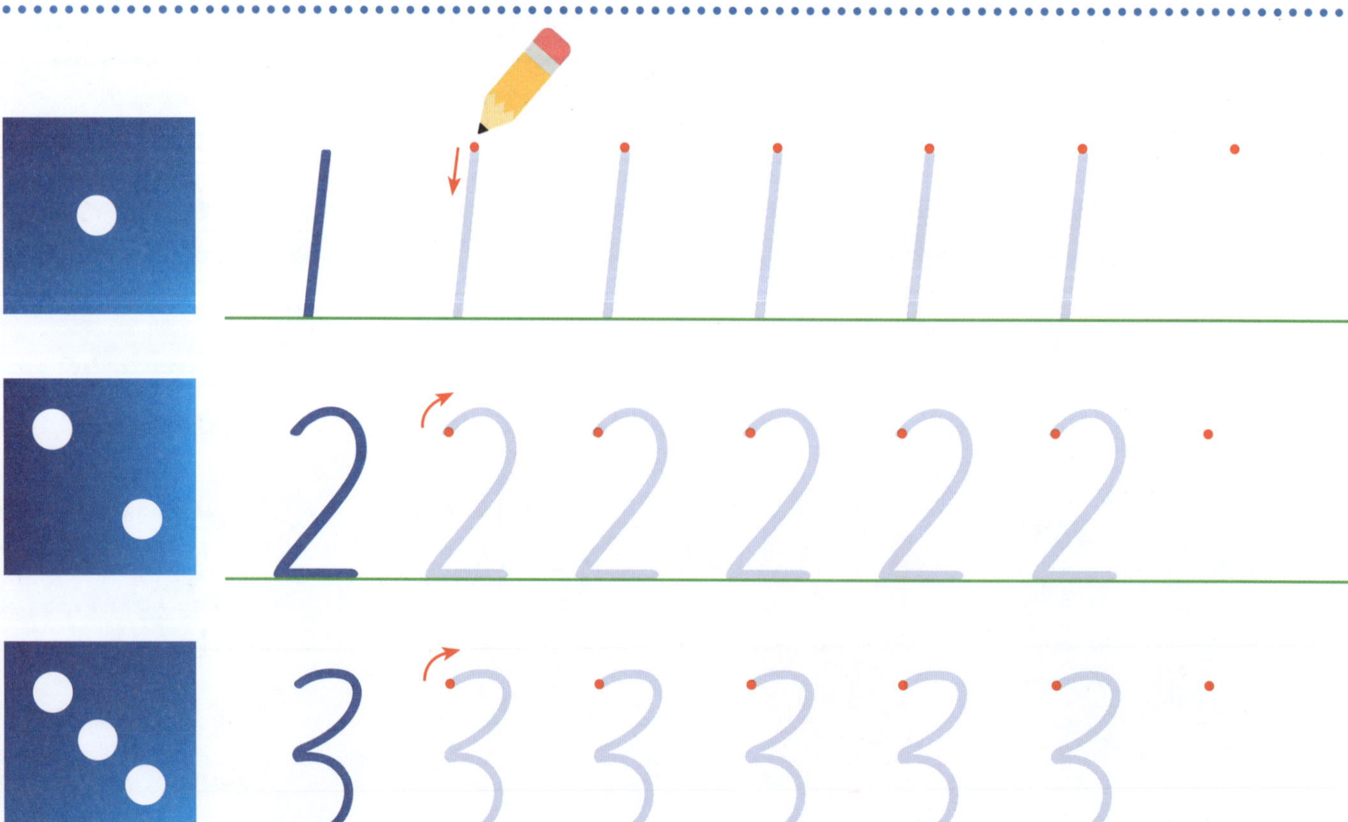



**Number • AC9MFN01** name, represent and order numbers to at least 20 • **AC9MFN02** recognise the number of objects within a collection using subitising

# Four, five

1 one 2 two 3 three 4 four 5 five

How many?

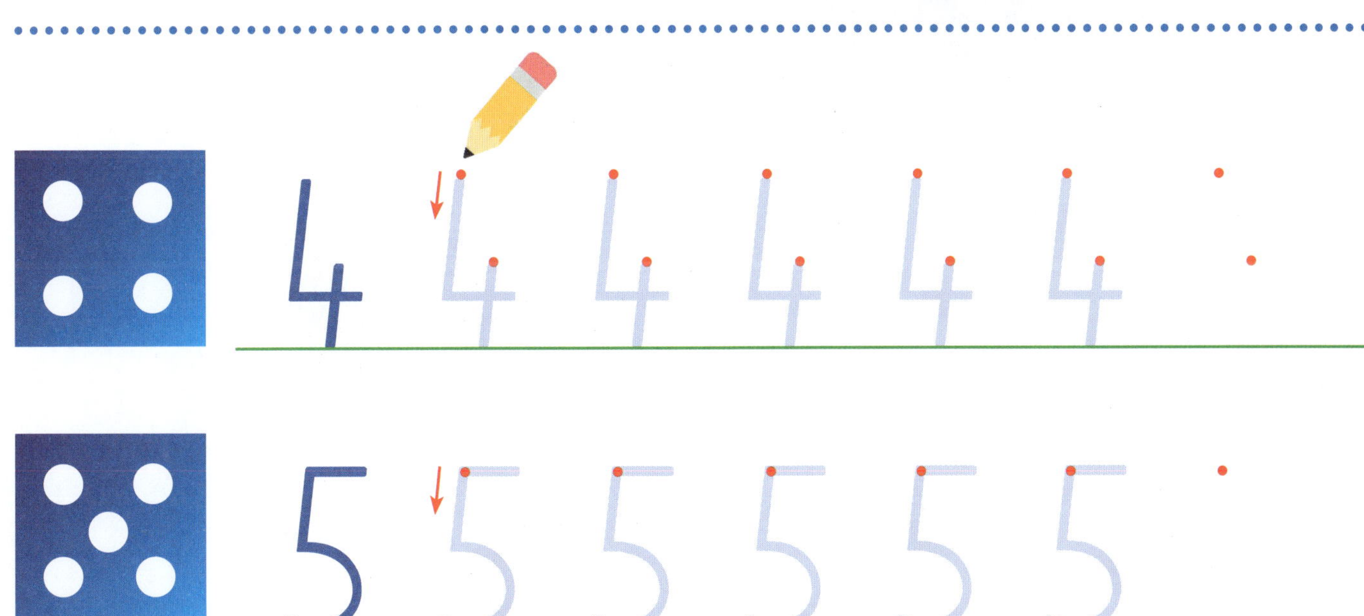

# Number names to five

How many?

1 2 3 4 5

one

two

three

four

five

**Number • AC9MFN01** name, represent and order numbers including zero to at least 20, using physical and virtual materials and numerals

# Counting back to zero

How many leaves?

How many cakes?

0 0 0 0 0 0

zero zero

# Six, seven, eight

Draw 8 legs and 7 spots.

How many?

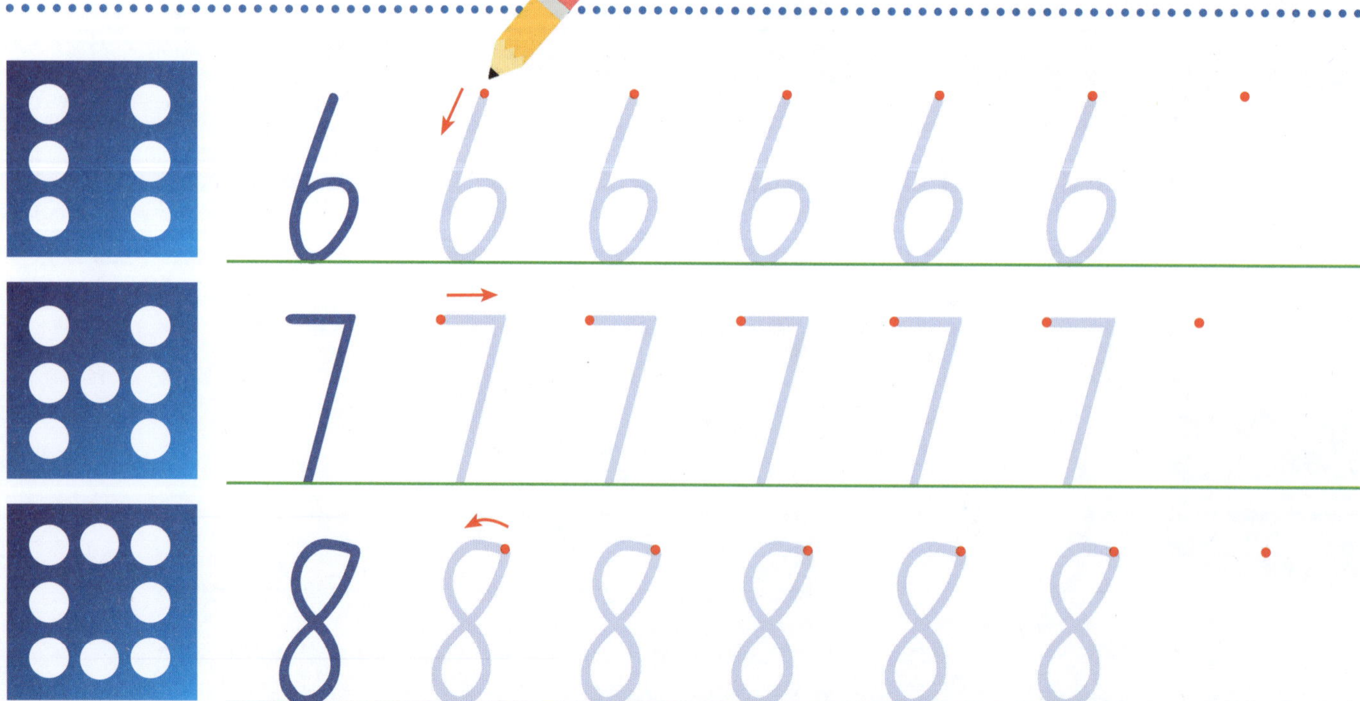



**Number** • **AC9MFN01** name, represent and order numbers to at least 20 • **AC9MFN02** recognise the number of objects within a collection using subitising

# Nine, ten

How many?

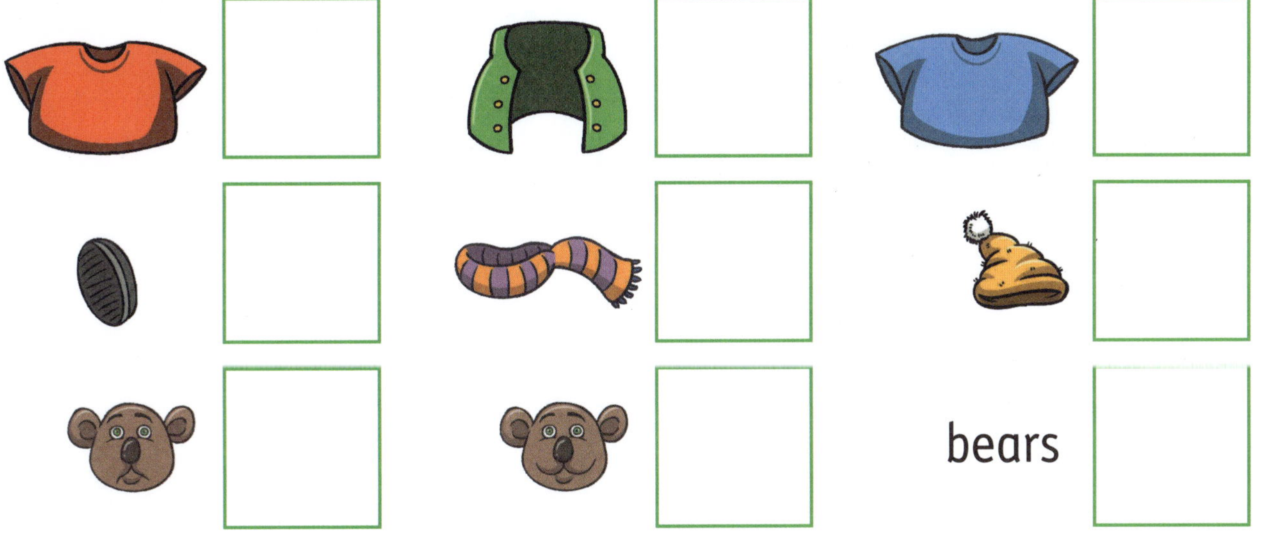


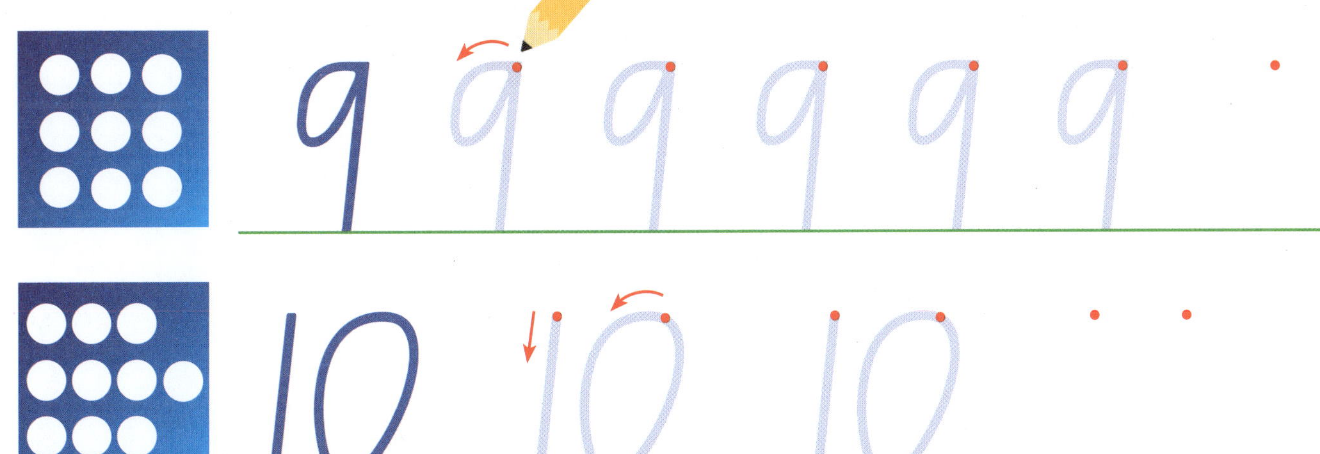

# Number names six to ten

How many?

six

seven

eight

nine

ten

## Mastery Checklist

I can:
- ☐ recognise dice and domino dot patterns.
- ☐ count the total number in a group to 10.
- ☐ read numerals to 10, including zero.
- ☐ show numbers using objects, words and numerals.

# Problem solving

## Ten fish

How can 10 fish be put into two fish bowls?

I can solve a problem by:

☐ counting to 10. ☐ drawing a picture.

# 2D shapes

Colour.

square

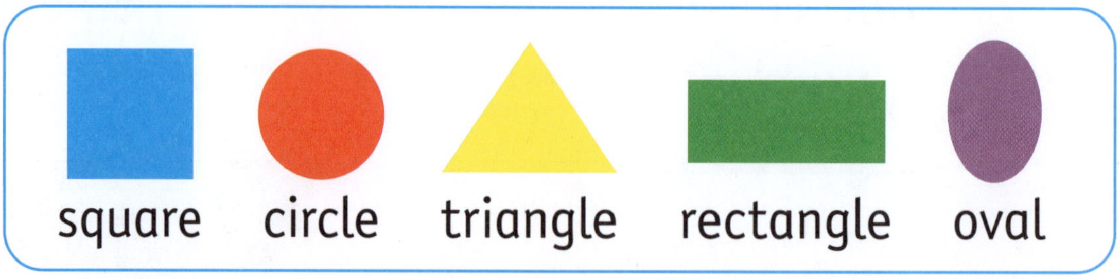

circle

triangle

rectangle

oval

**Space • AC9MFSP01** sort, name and create familiar shapes; recognise and describe familiar shapes within objects in the environment, giving reasons

# 2D shapes

Match.

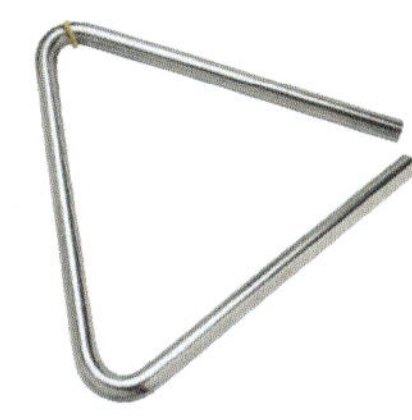

square

circle

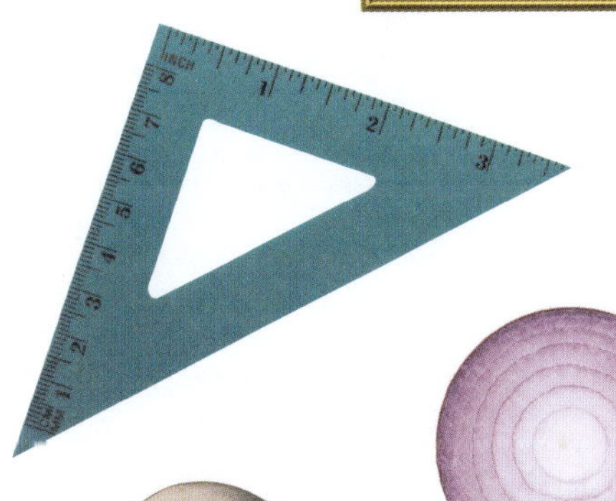

triangle

rectangle

oval

# Patterns with shapes

Colour to repeat the pattern.

Colour to make a pattern.

# Closed shapes and lines

Colour all the closed shapes.
Tick ✓ the curved lines.

**closed shape** □
**curved line** ∿

**Explore** Draw a zigzag with straight lines.
Draw and describe other shapes.

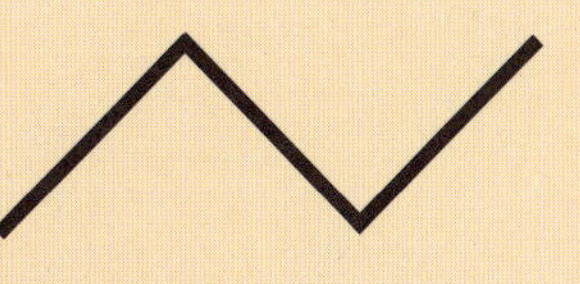

# Problem solving

## Addition

Draw and add.

| | |
|---|---|
| 3 more balls. | How many balls? |
| 3 more fish. | How many fish? |
| 4 more blocks. | How many blocks? |
| 1 more teddy. | How many teddies? |

I can solve problems by:

☐ counting on to add. ☐ drawing a picture.

# Addition to five

1

4 and ___

2

3 and ___

3

4

**Challenge!** How many red?  How many blue? ☐

# Combinations to 3, 4 and 5

Use counters to help you.

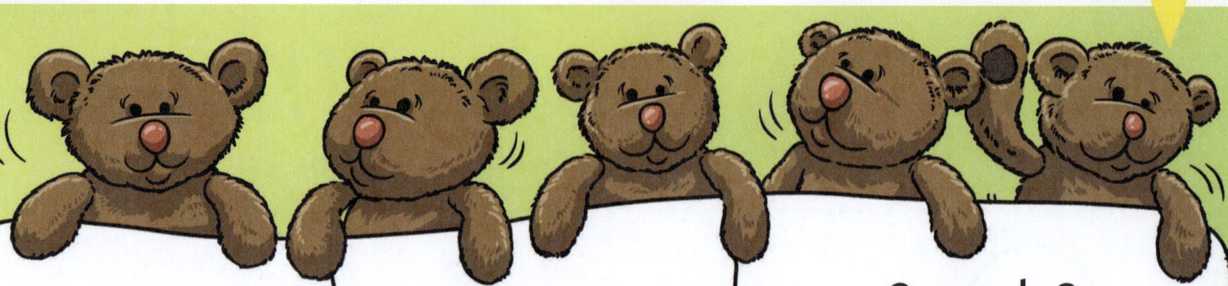

2 and 1

4 and 0

3 and 2

2 and 3

1 and 2

3 and 0

3 and 1 more

4 and 1 more

5 add 0

2 add 2

1 add 3

**Challenge!**

Draw dominoes with 6 spots.
Make each one different.

# Making numbers using five

Draw more dots to match the number.

7 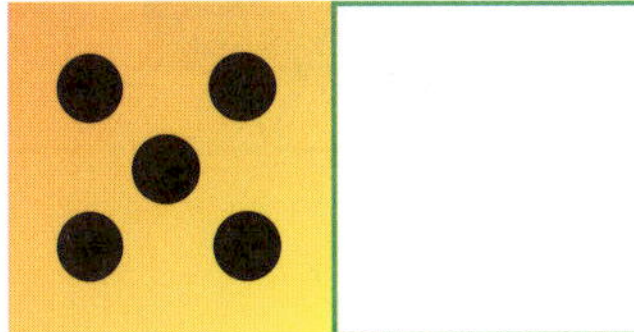

5 + ____

6 

____ + ____

10 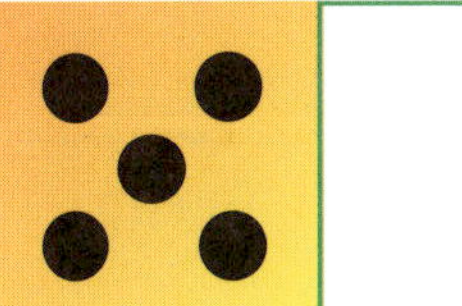

____ + ____

8 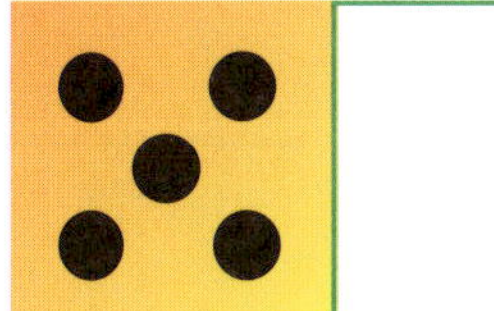

____ + ____

9 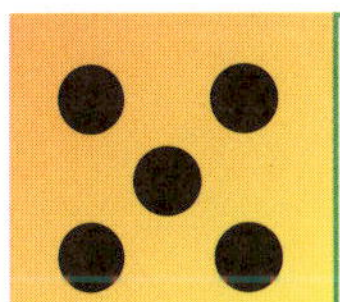

____ + ____

5 

____ + ____

**Challenge!**
How many dots did you draw altogether?

## Mastery Checklist

I can:

- ☐ identify familiar shapes, lines and curves.
- ☐ make repeating patterns using shapes.
- ☐ combine groups and find the total.
- ☐ use five when making numbers from six to ten.

# One to ten

Investigation 1

Choose a number between 1 and 10.

My number is ____________

Draw it in 4 different ways.

Where have you seen your number?

______________________________

______________________________

______________________________

# One to ten

Investigation 1

Choose another number. Write it in the circle.

Tell us everything you can about this number.

Draw and write.

To do this, I needed to:

- [ ] write numbers as quantities.
- [ ] write numbers in numerals.
- [ ] write numbers in words.

I enjoyed this task! ☆☆☆☆☆

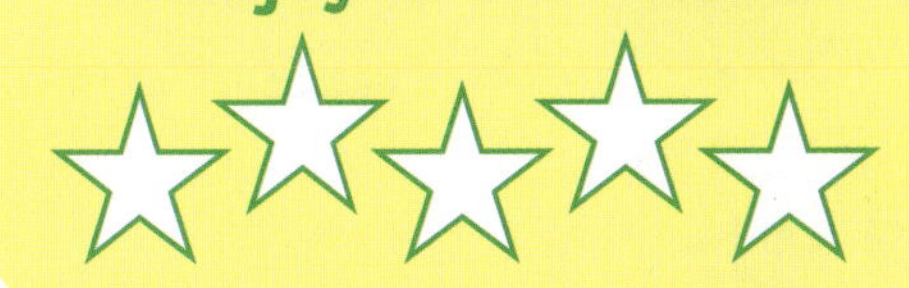

# Revision

## 1 Draw each path.

| | | |
|---|---|---|
| 2 | two | 5 |
| 3 | five | 2 |
| 4 | three | 4 |
| 5 | four | 3 |
| 6 | six | 6 |

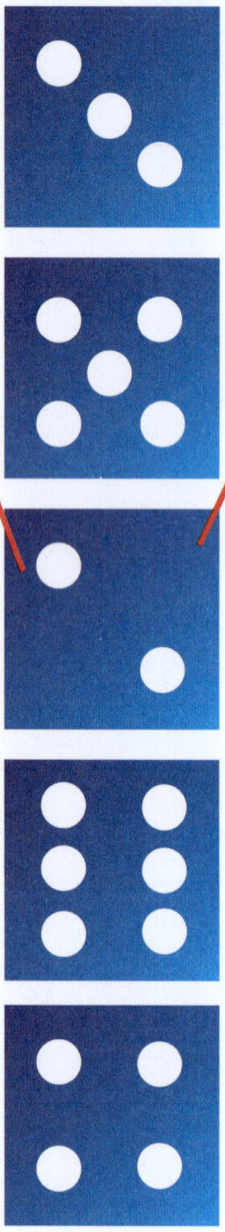

## 2 Colour.

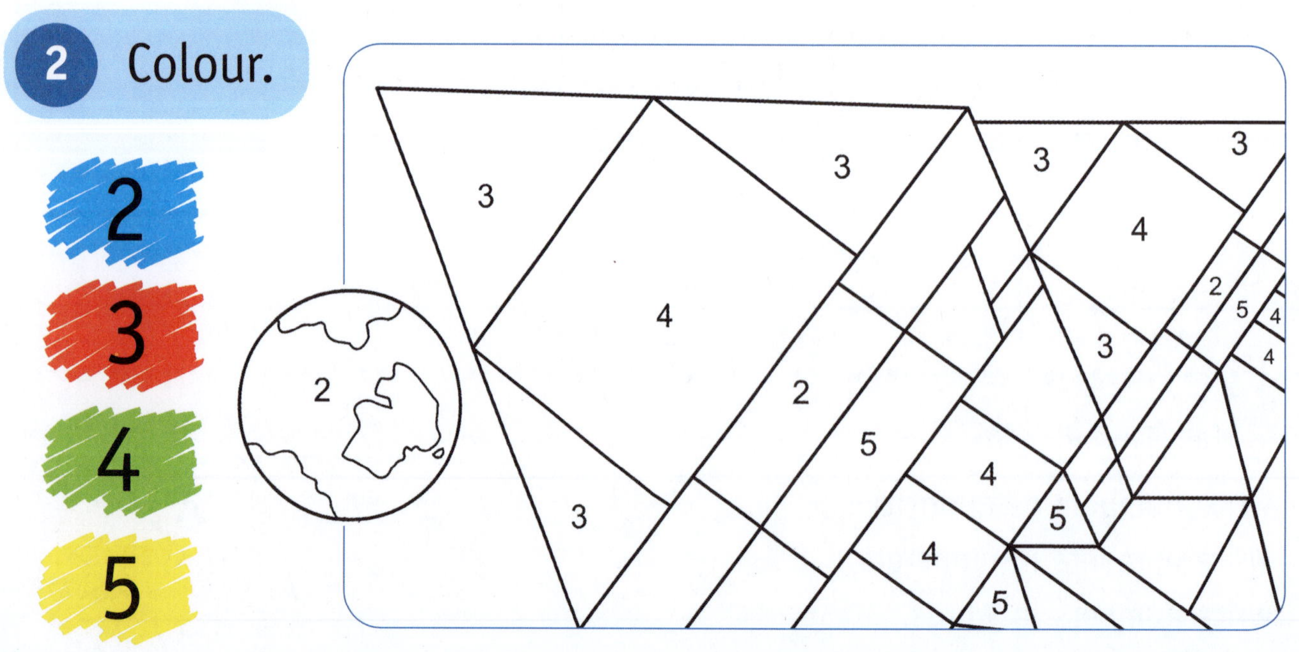

# Revision

3 Circle shapes that are:
square
triangle
circle
rectangle
AUSTRALIA
10
oval

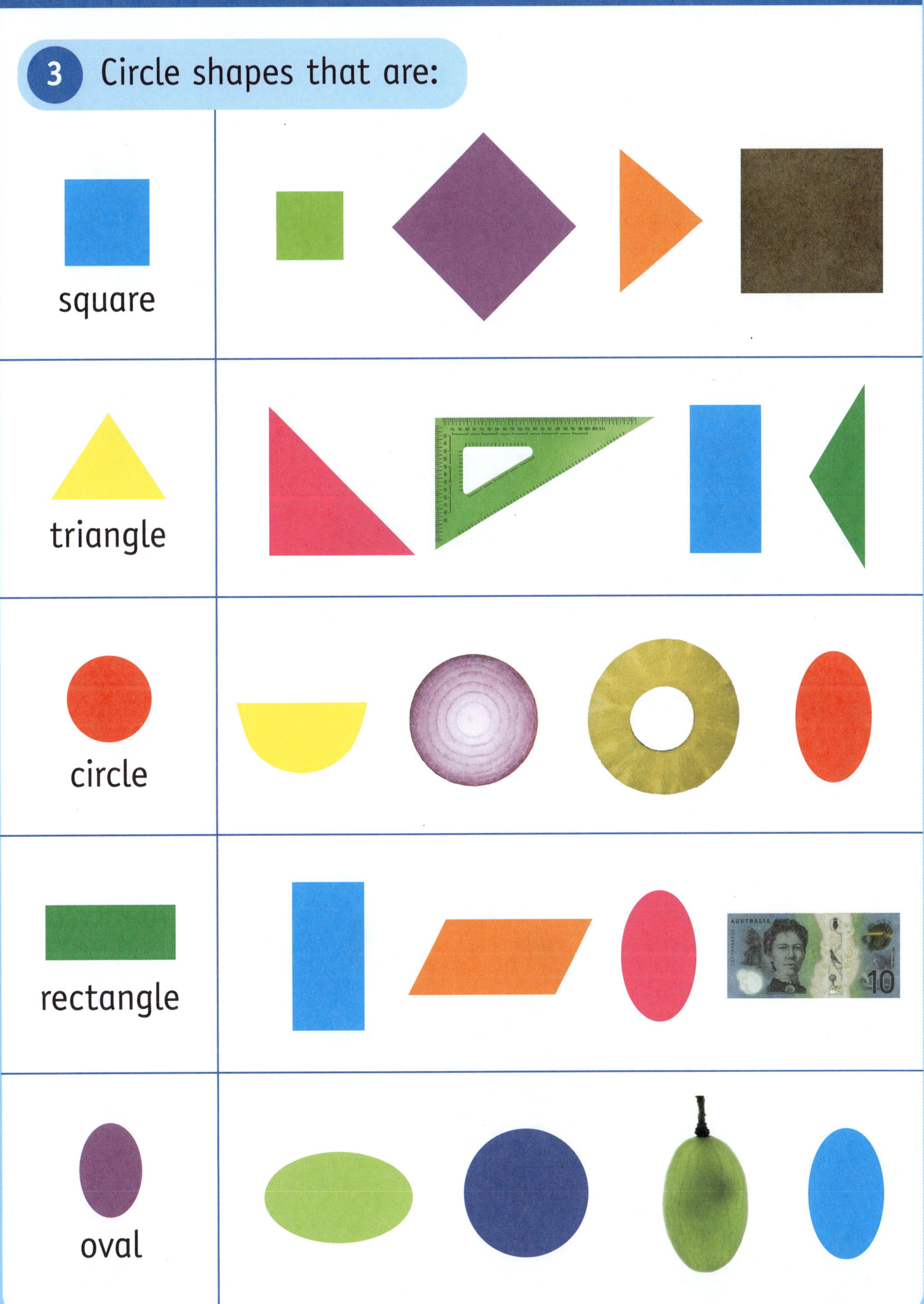

# Day and night

Match.

night time

daytime

night time

Draw something you do

before lunch

after lunch

morning

afternoon

# Longer and shorter time

Tick ✓ the one that takes **longer**.

Draw something that takes a long time.

Circle the one that takes a **shorter** time.

# Yesterday, today and tomorrow

Time 

Colour today **blue**.

Sunday

Monday

Tuesday

Wednesday

Thursday

Friday

Saturday

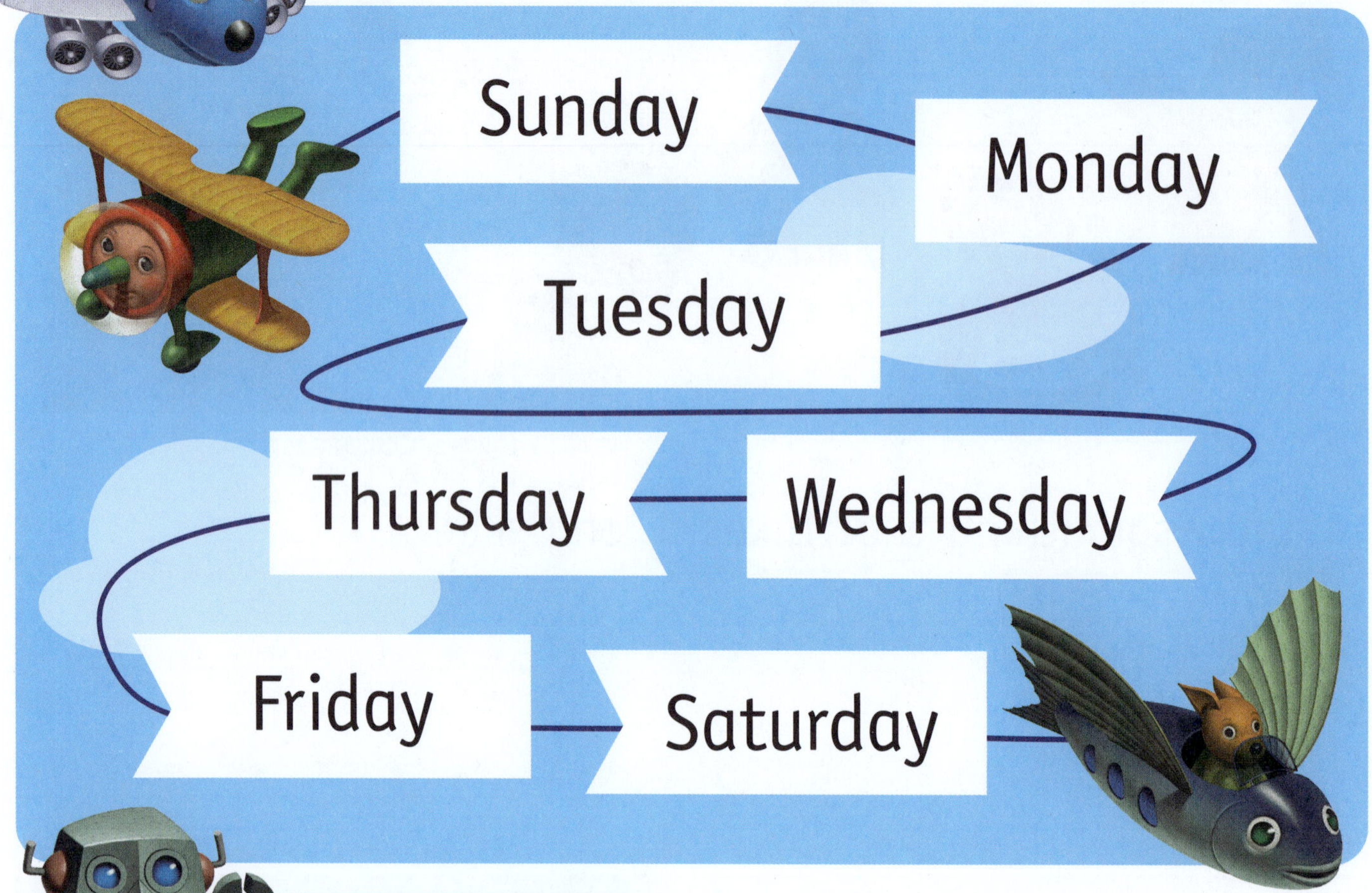

Draw a picture.

| Yesterday | Tomorrow |
|---|---|
| | |
| What day was yesterday? Colour yesterday **red**. | What day is tomorrow? Colour tomorrow **green**. |

# Days of the week

## Weekdays

What do you do each day?

Monday

Tuesday

Wednesday

Thursday

Friday

## Weekend days

Saturday

Sunday

## Mastery Checklist

I can:

- ☐ use words such as daytime, night time, morning, afternoon, today, tomorrow, yesterday, before, after.
- ☐ compare how long things take.
- ☐ link events to a day of the week.

# Subtraction stories

**Subtract =**
**Take some away.**

**1** 4 fish.
1 swims away.

How many left?

**2** 3 cats.
2 run away.

How many left?

**3** 4 bikes.
2 ride away.

How many left?

**4** 5 cars.
2 drive away.

How many left?

**Challenge!** 8 mice. 3 run away.

How many left?

# Take away



Take away 1.

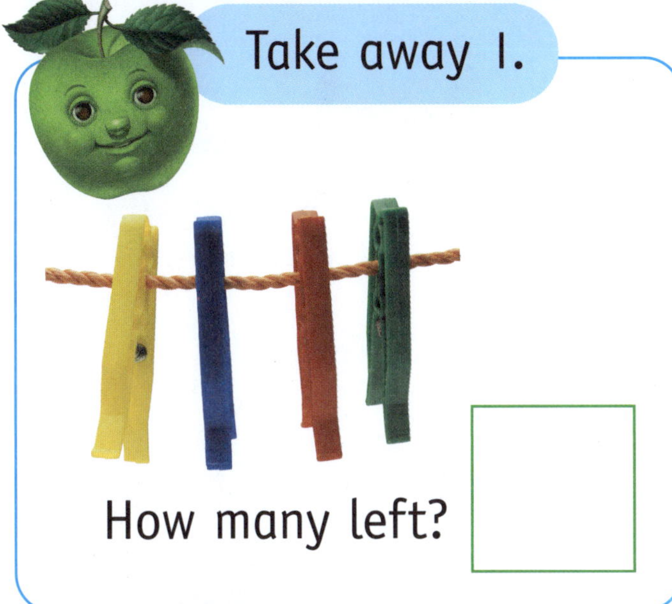

How many left? ☐

How many left? ☐

Take away 2.

How many left? ☐

How many left? ☐

Match.

4 take away 1 | 3 take away 2 | 5 take away 1

| 0 | 1 | 2 | 3 | 4 | 5 |
|---|---|---|---|---|---|

2 take away 2 | 4 take away 2 | 7 take away 2

# Heavy and light

Cross the heavy things.
Circle the light things.

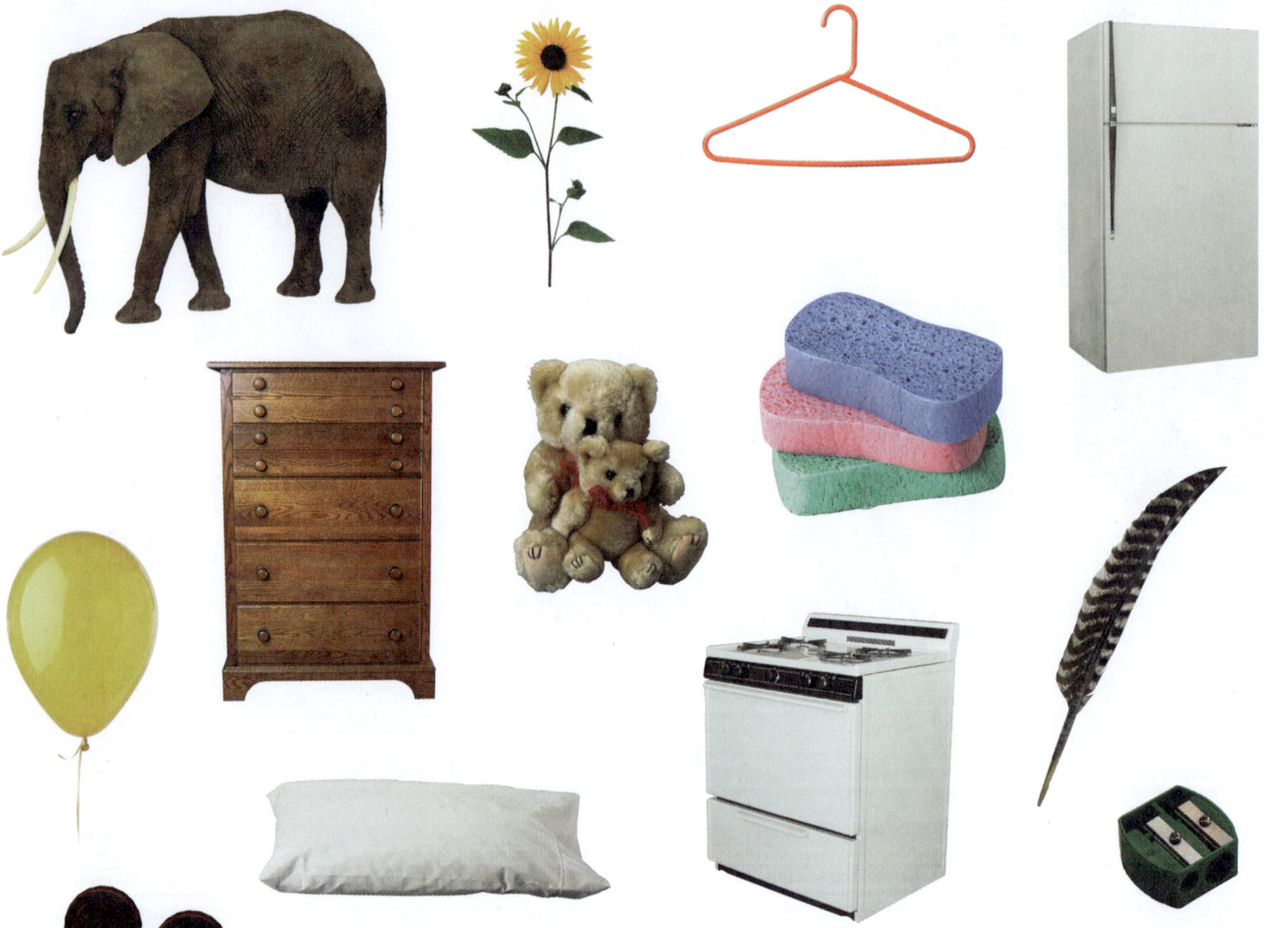

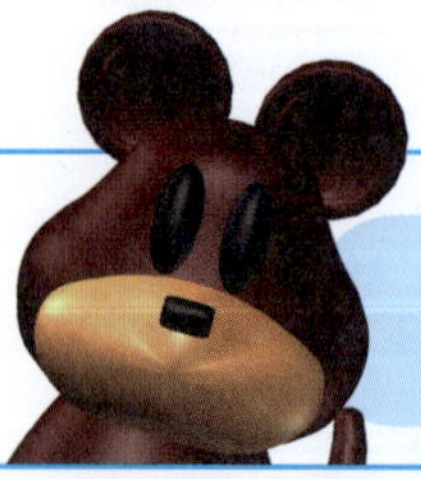

Circle.

# Light, heavier, heaviest

Match.

light

heavier

heaviest

Draw baby bear on his chair. Draw Mama bear on her bed.

## Mastery Checklist

I can:
- ☐ use diagrams to help with separating quantities.
- ☐ separate and take away part of a group to show subtraction.
- ☐ identify that objects can be heavy or light.
- ☐ compare masses.

# Halves

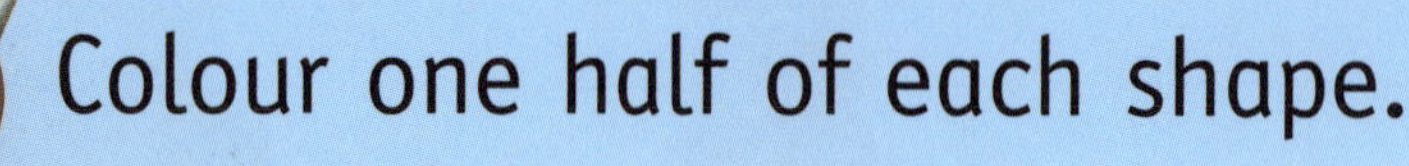


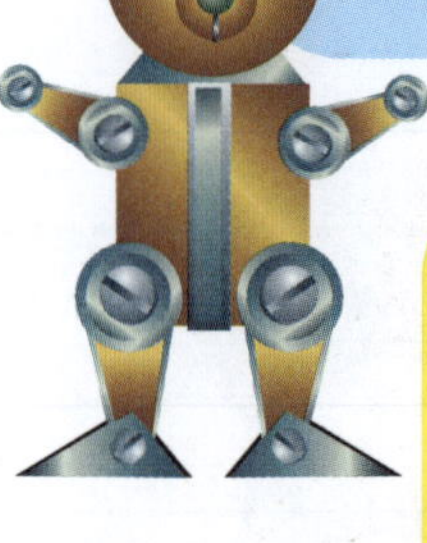

**Halves** are two equal parts.

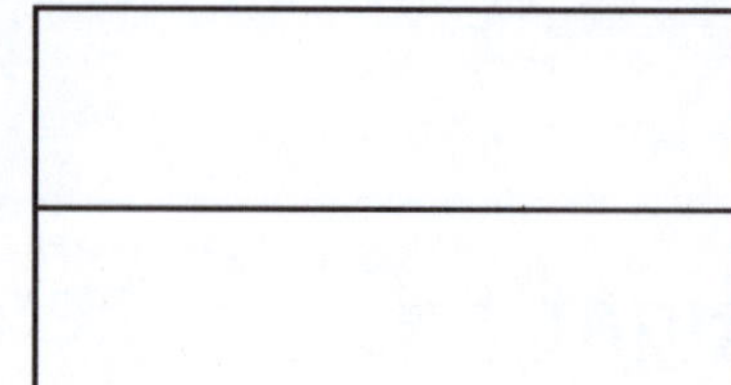

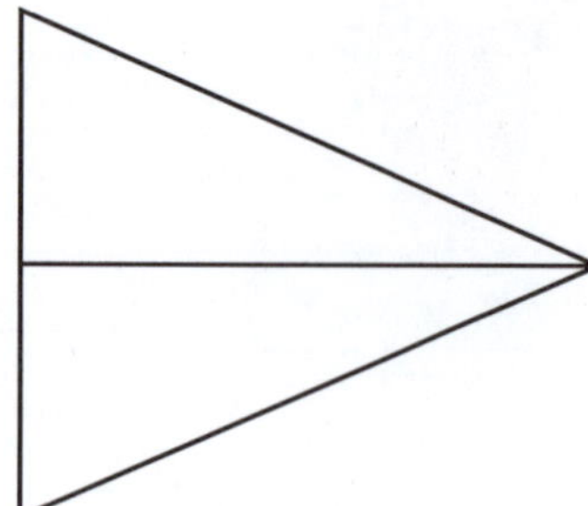

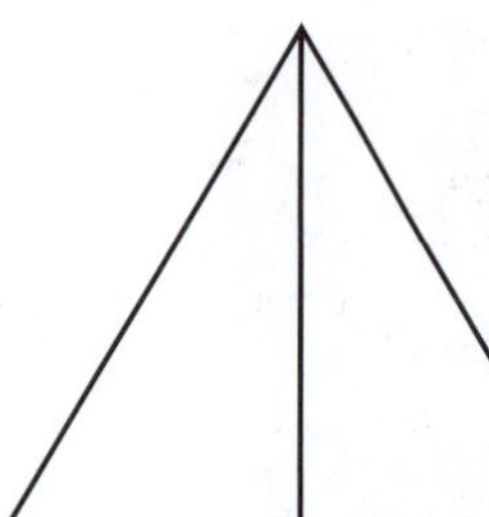

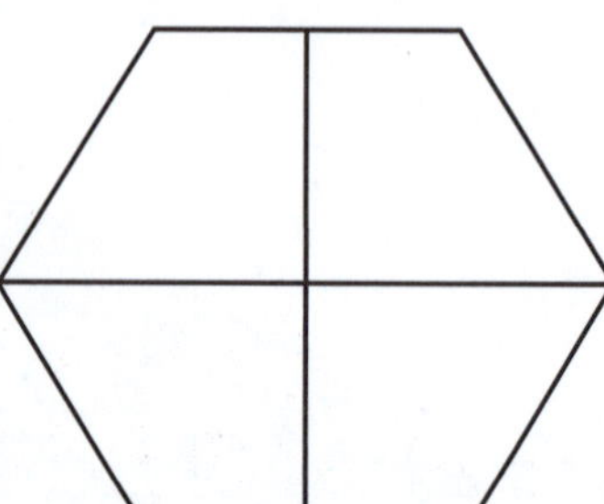

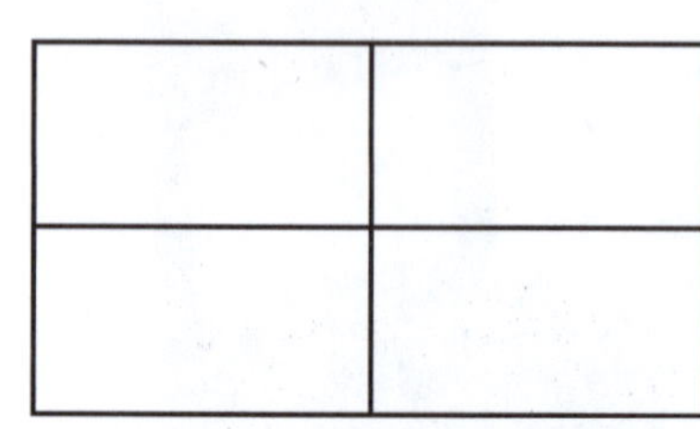

Tick ✓ shapes that are cut in half.

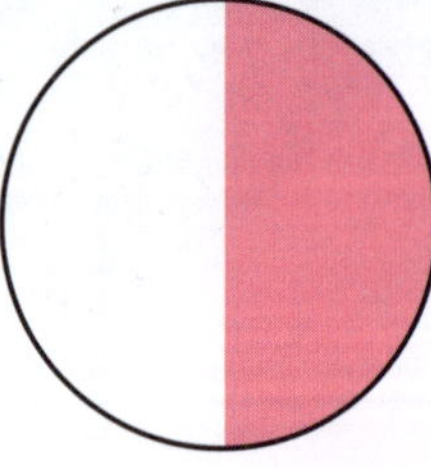

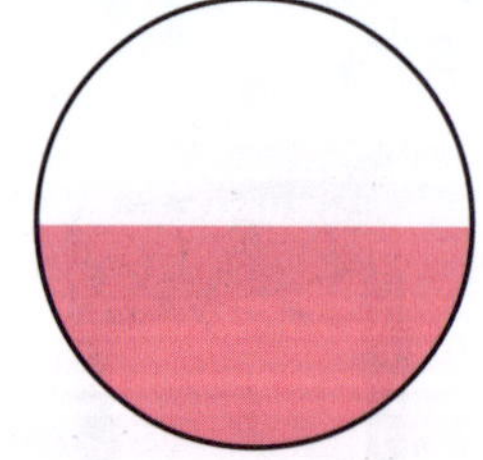

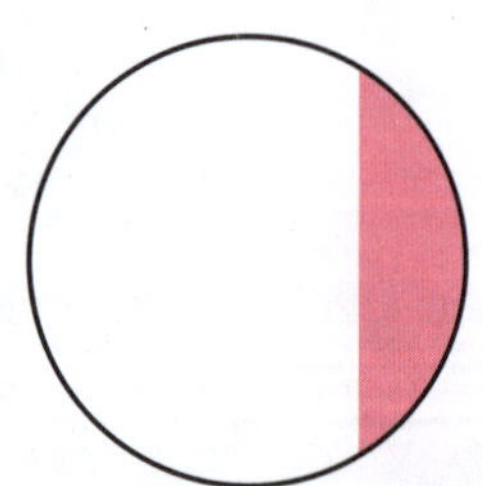

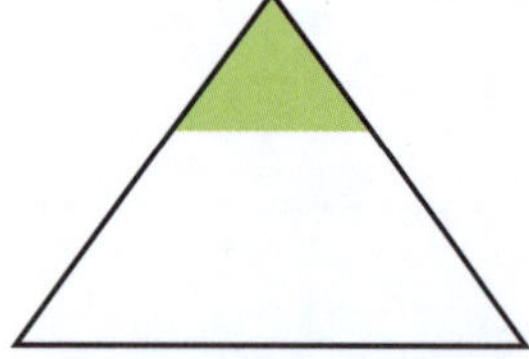

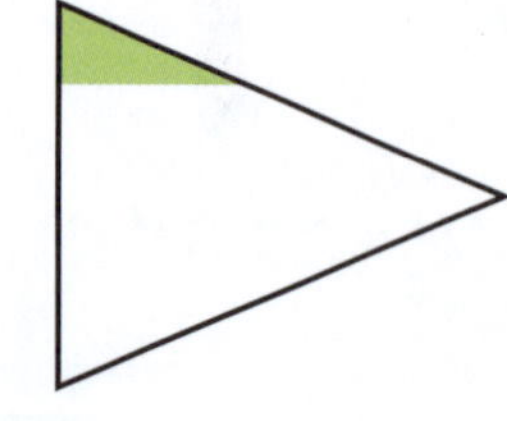

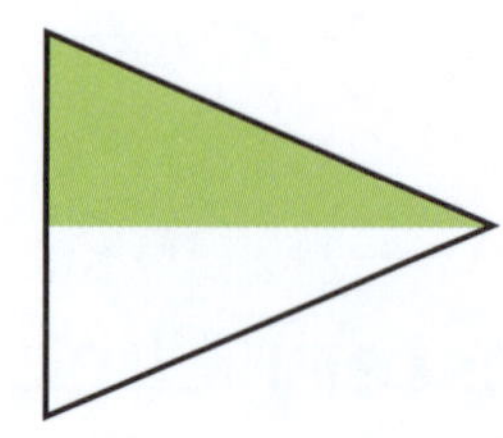

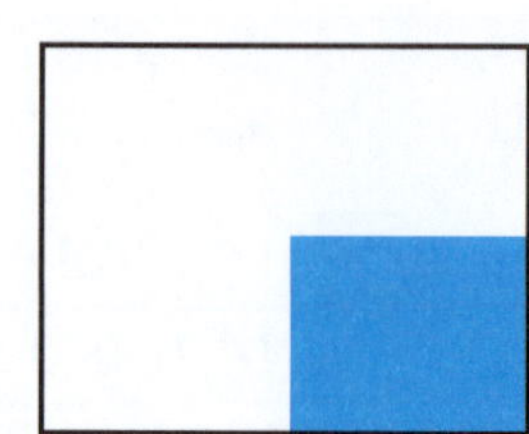

# Halves



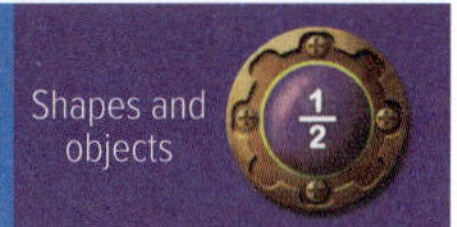

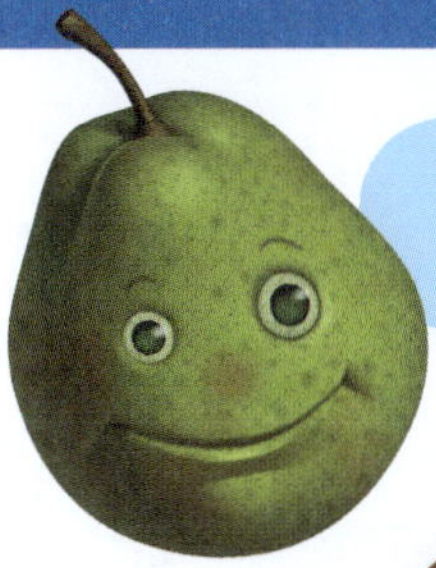

Circle the halves.

Circle the glass that is half full.

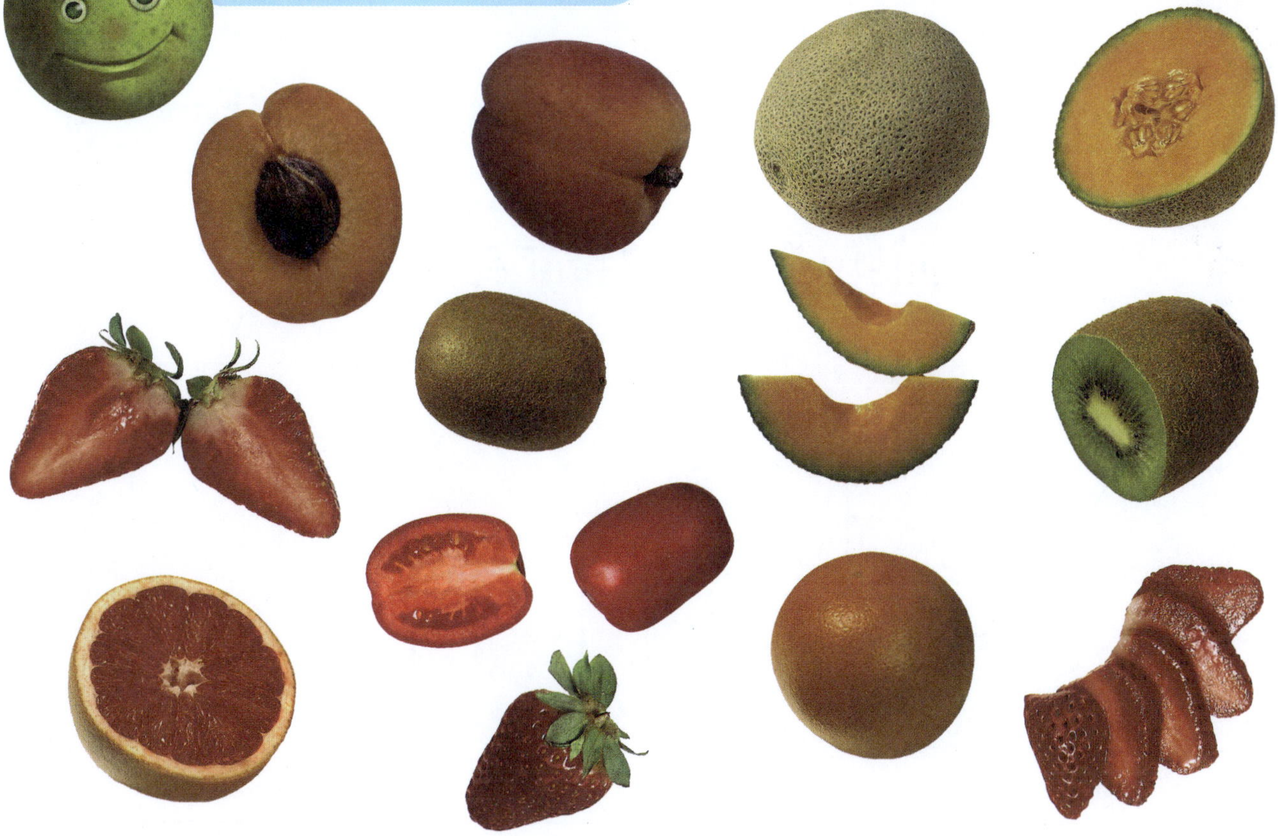

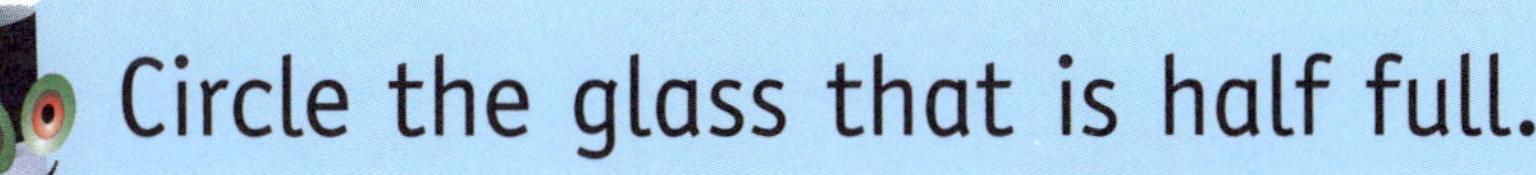

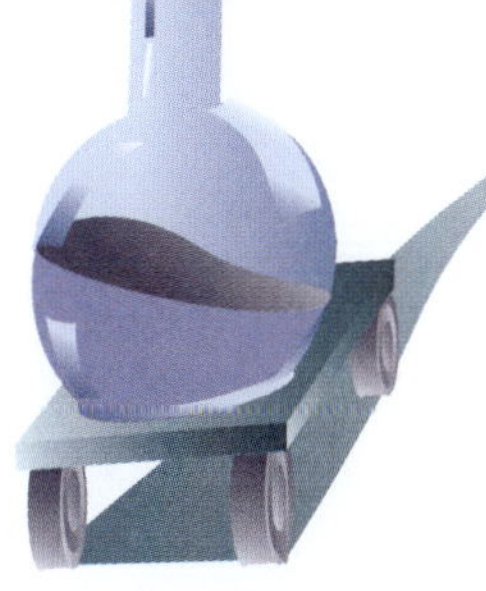

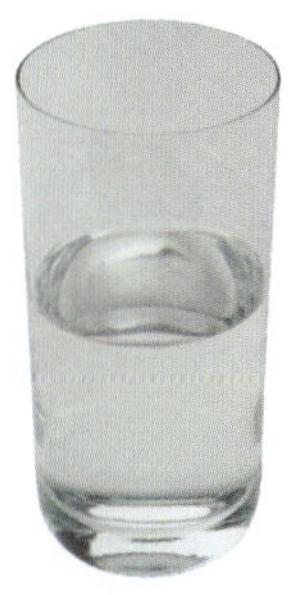

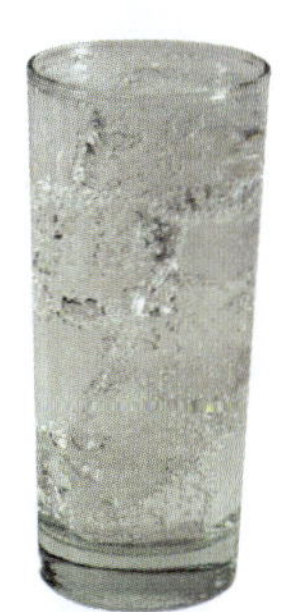

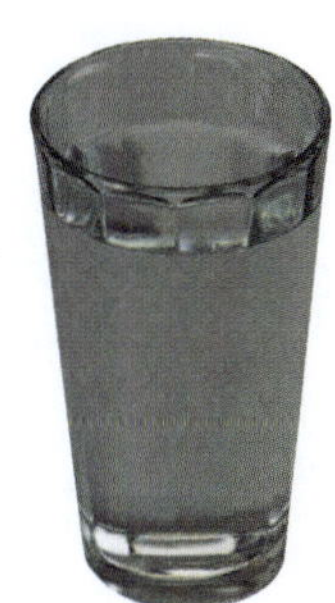

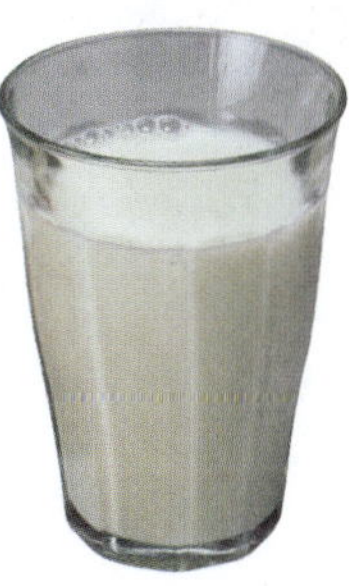

Circle the arrow that is halfway.

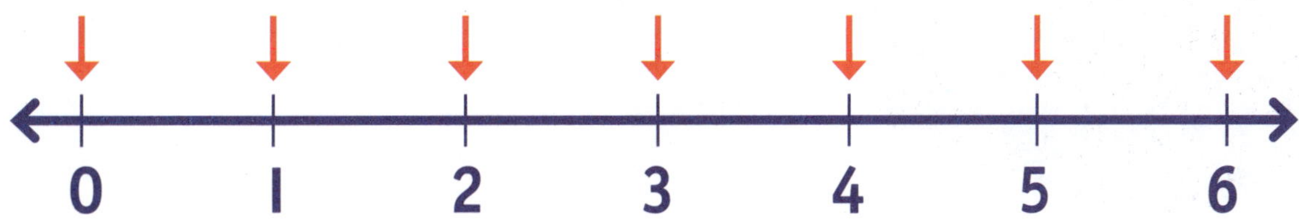

# Full, empty and half full

Match.

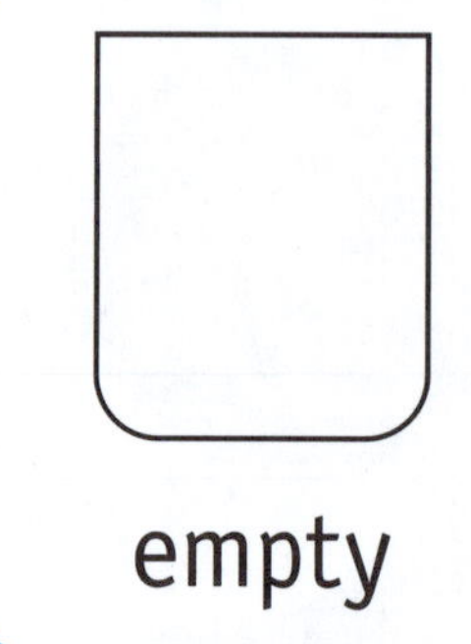

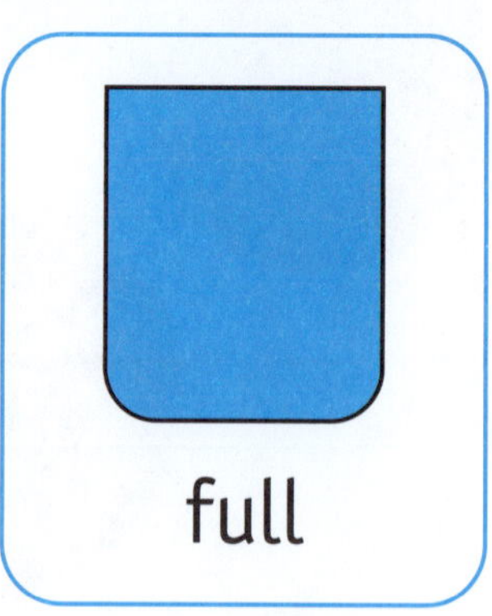


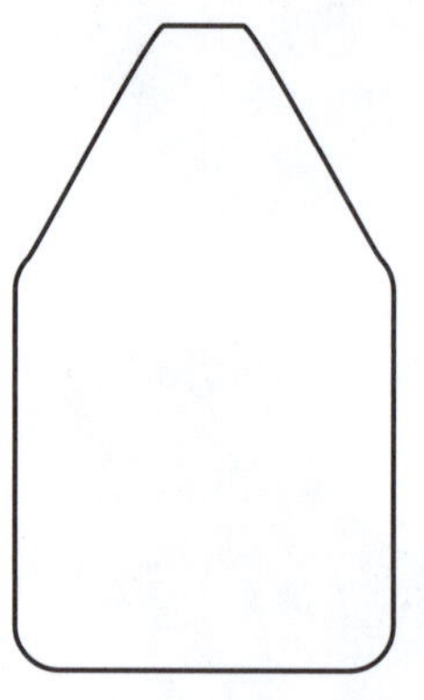

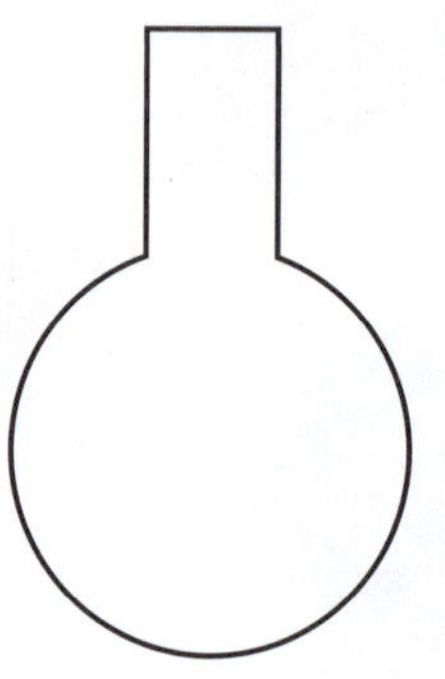

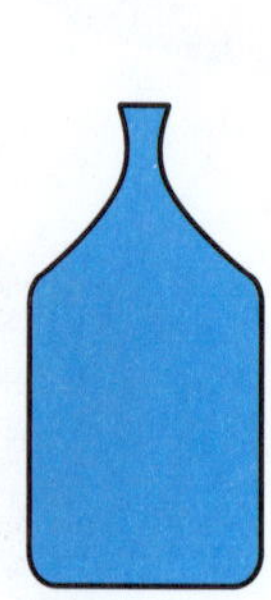

Colour.

full

O holds most. X holds least.

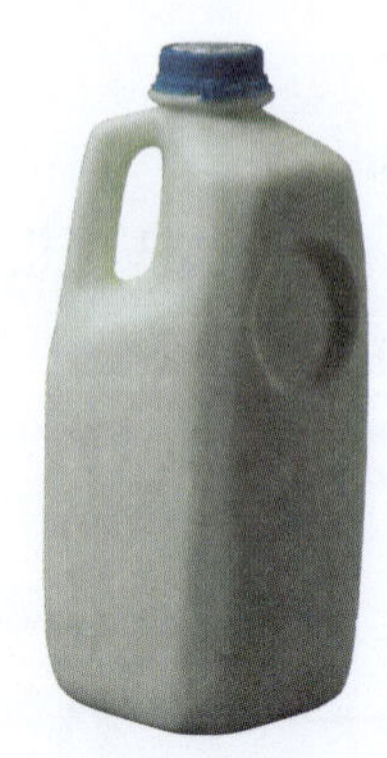

# Comparing capacities

Colour the number of  that fill each one.

**Capacity =**
**How much does it hold?**

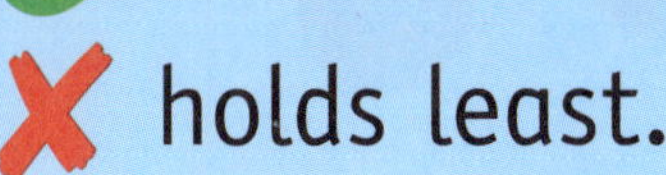 holds most.
holds least.

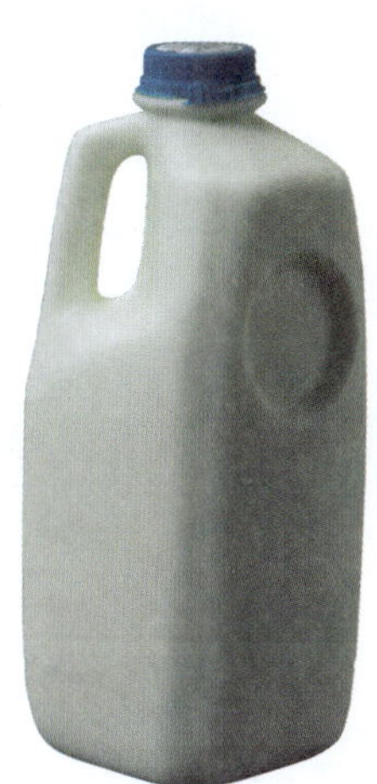

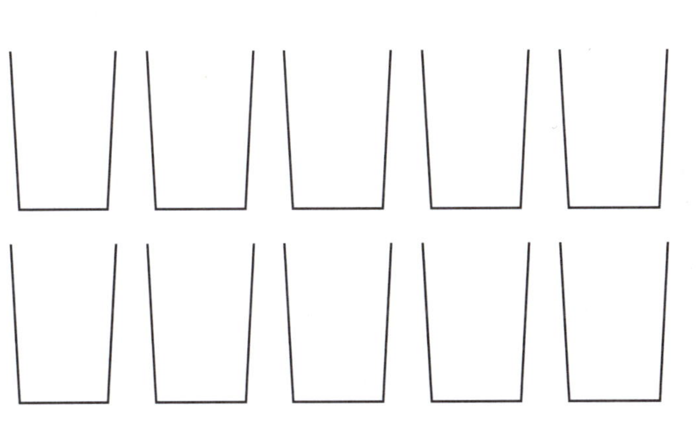

## Mastery Checklist

I can:

- [ ] cut a length into two equal parts.
- [ ] find the halfway point.
- [ ] use the terms 'full', 'empty' and 'about half full'.
- [ ] fill and empty containers.

# Revision • Term 1

## 1 How many?

## 2 Write the numerals.

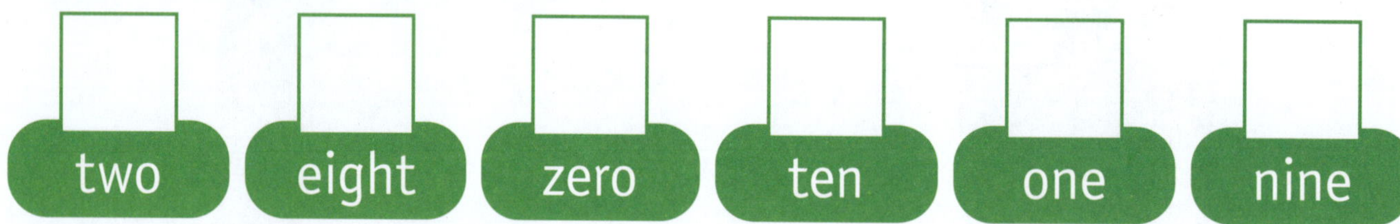


## 3 Write the word.

3 

4 

## 4 Match.

triangle rectangle square circle

5 Colour one half of each shape.

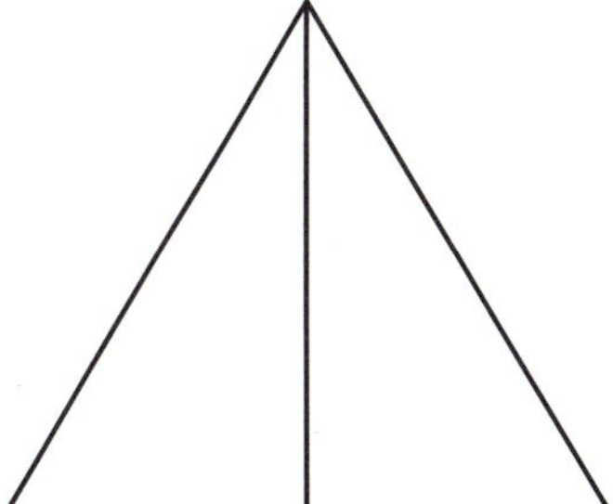
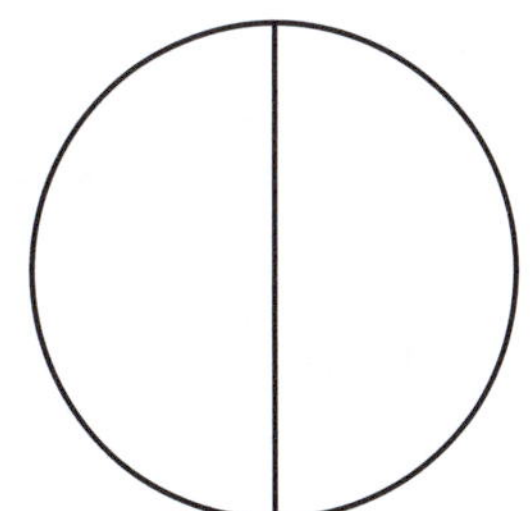
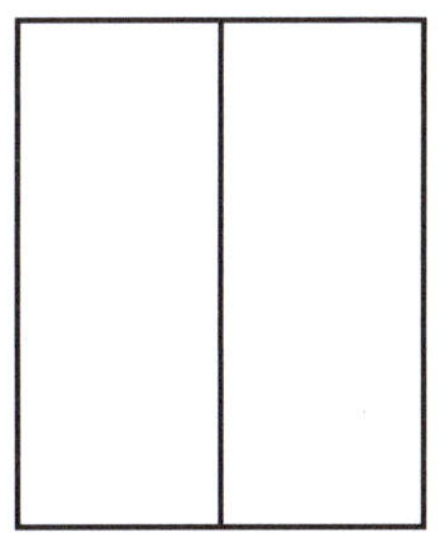

6 Circle the one that holds the most.

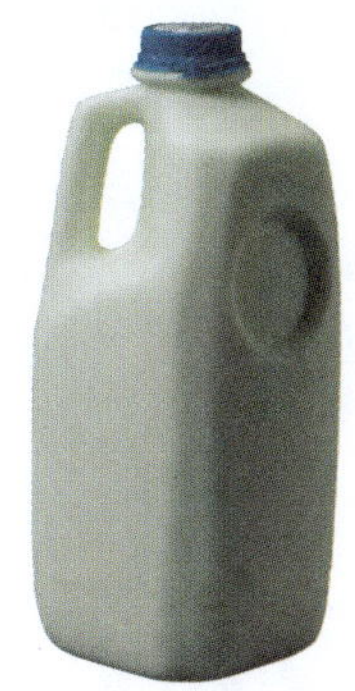

Cross the one that holds the least.

7 Draw lines to match.

| | |
|---|---|
| | Monday |
| | Tuesday |
| Thursday | |
| | |
| Saturday | Friday |
| | |
| Wednesday | Sunday |

# Counting to twenty

Match flower beds to numbers. Write the missing numbers.

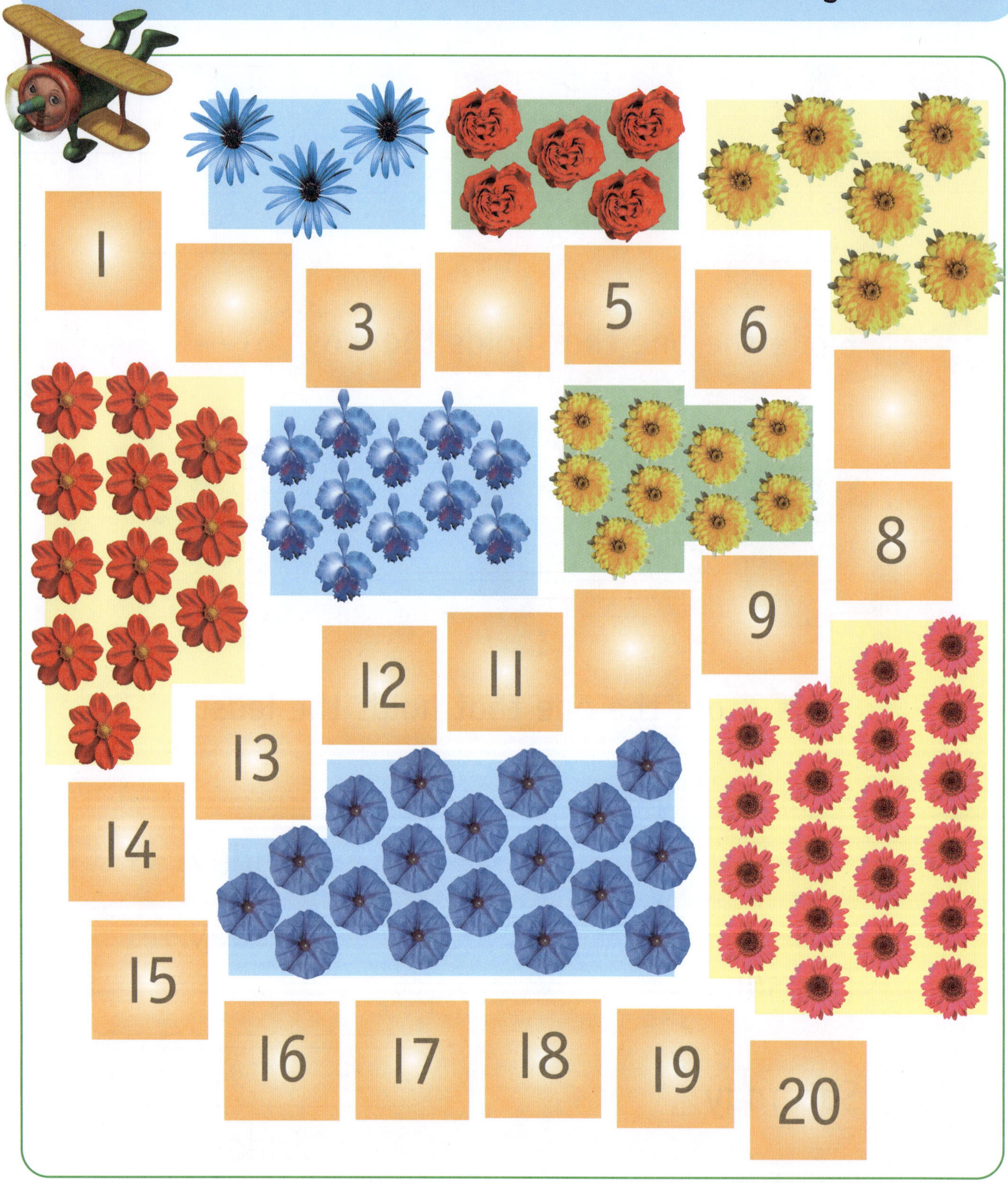

1

3

5

6

8

9

12

11

13

14

15

16

17

18

19

20

**Challenge!**

How many? Red flowers ☐ Blue flowers ☐



**Number • AC9MFN01** name, represent and order numbers including zero to at least 20, using physical and virtual materials and numerals

# Counting back from ten

Write the missing numbers. Count back.

10 9

9 8 5

10 7 5 3 0

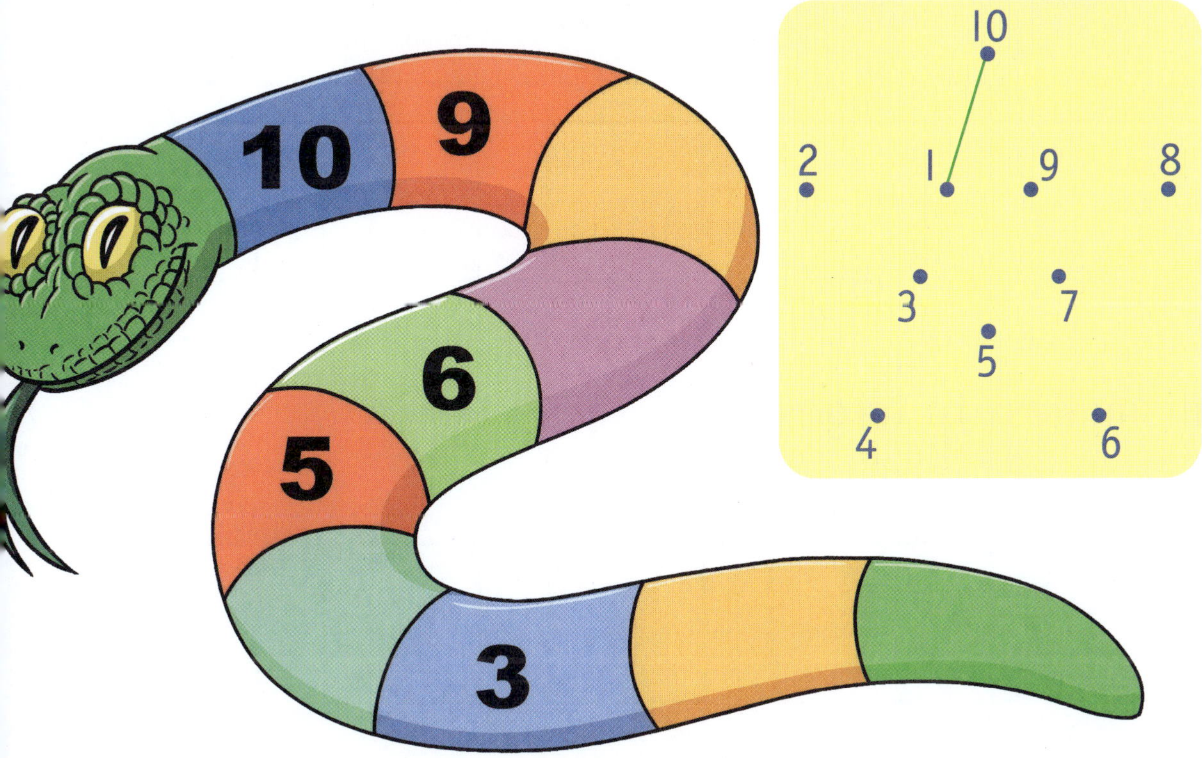

10 9 6 5 3

10, 2, 1, 9, 8, 3, 7, 5, 4, 6

**Challenge!**

How many cars on two trucks?

# Ordering numbers to ten

How many?

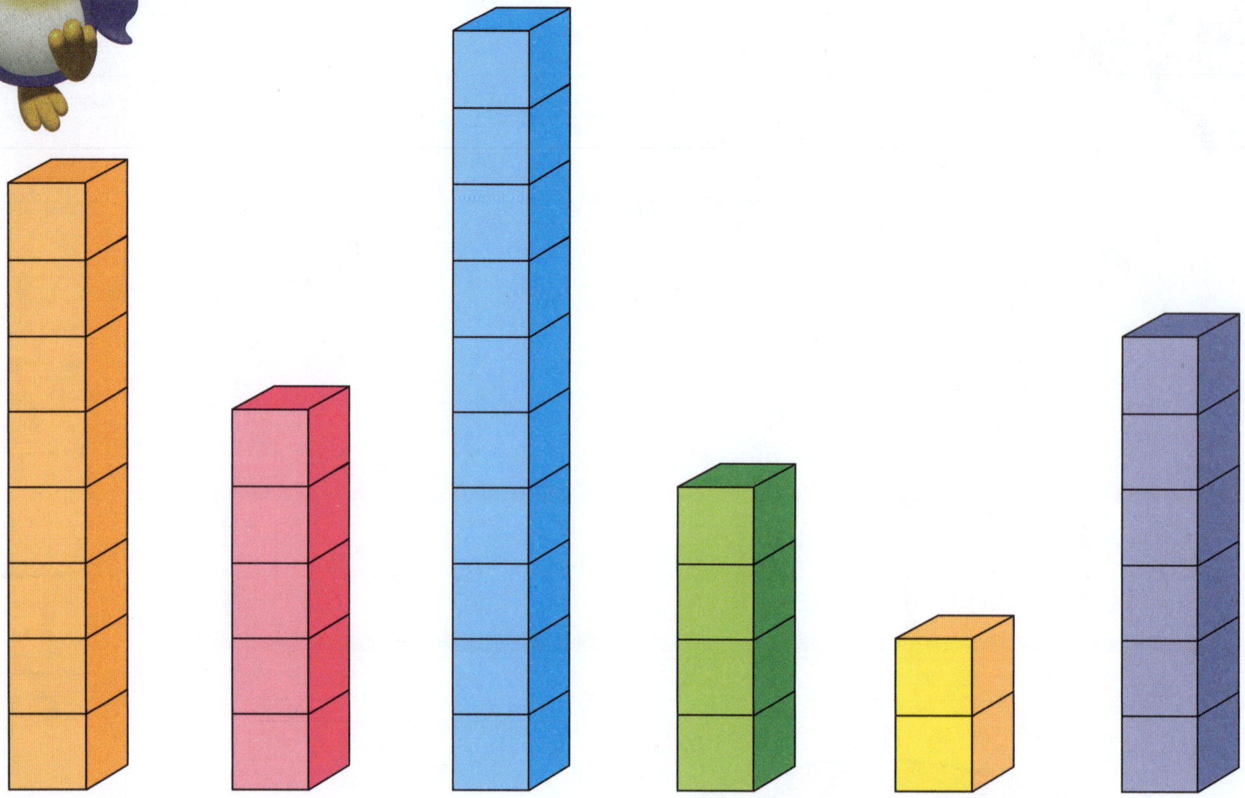

Order from smallest to largest.

smallest

largest

**Challenge!**

What are the missing numbers?

**Number** • **AC9MFN01** name, represent and order numbers to at least 20 • **AC9MFN03** quantify and compare collections to at least 20

# Ordering numbers to ten

## Write the numbers in order.

1 3 5 2 4 ____________

2 6 5 8 7 ____________

3 9 8 7 10 ____________

4 3 7 10 4 ____________

## Make and order.

## Mastery Checklist

I can:
- ☐ count forwards to 20 and backwards from 10.
- ☐ count the total number in a group to 20.
- ☐ read numerals to 20, including zero.
- ☐ order numbers to 10.

# Adding

Add to 10

 and  makes 

and makes 

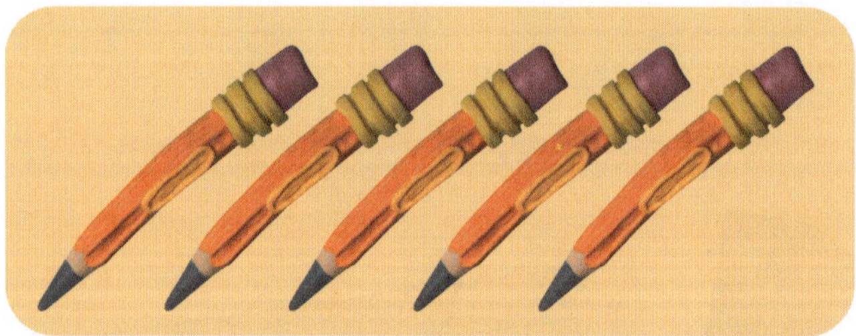
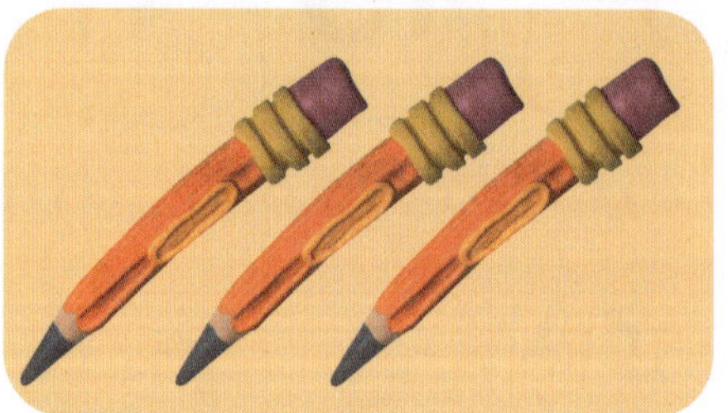

and makes 

and makes 

**Number • AC9MFN05** represent practical situations involving addition, subtraction and quantification with physical and virtual materials and use counting or subitising strategies

# Counting on

5 and 2 more

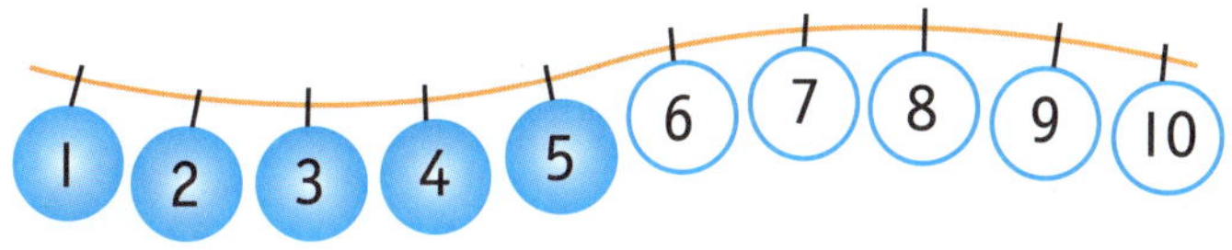


4 and 3 more

6 and 2 more

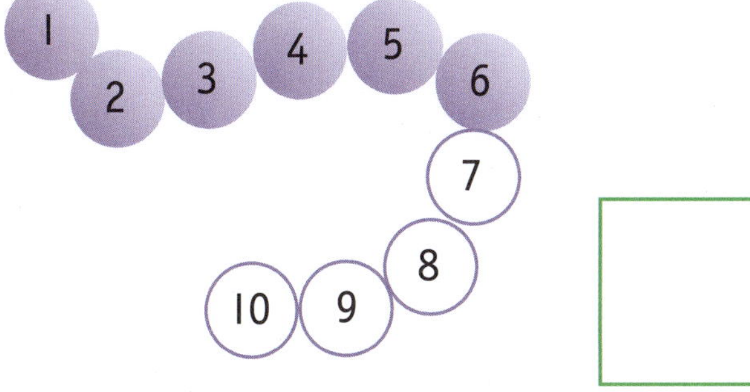


5 and 3 more

7 and 3 more

8 and 2 more

## Challenge!

and three more and three more and three more

# Combinations to 10

How many more to make 10?

You can use counters.

1

2

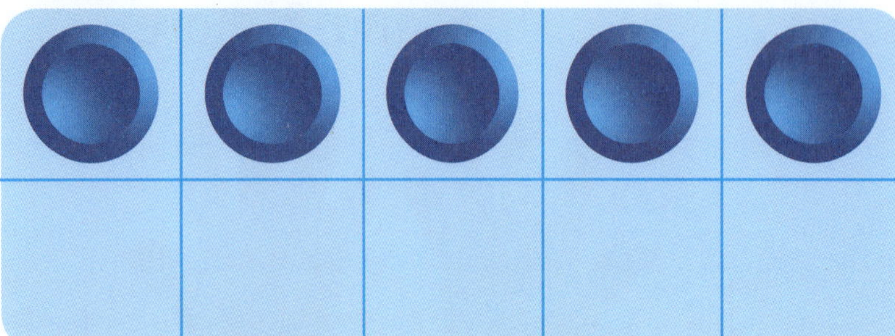

3

4

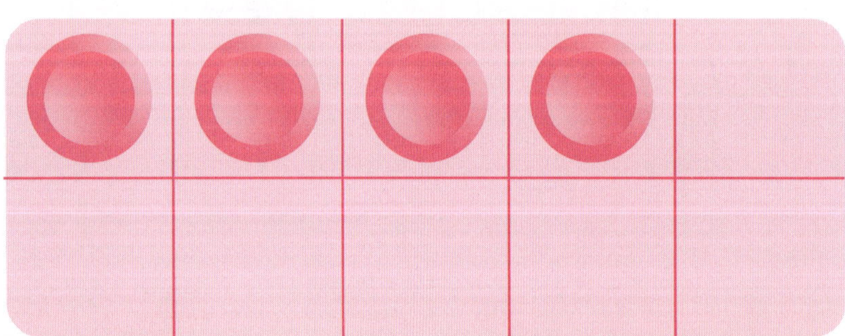

**Explore** Find other ways to make 10.

**Number • AC9MFN04** partition and combine collections up to 10 using part-part-whole relationships and subitising to recognise and name the parts

# Problem solving

## Animal zoo

Where do the animals live? Draw them.

**Challenge!** How many altogether?

animals ☐ eyes ☐ legs ☐

I can solve a problem by:

☐ adding groups together. ☐ drawing a picture.

# Tallest and shortest

Circle.

the tallest

the highest

the shortest

the lowest

Draw.

a shorter boy

a taller girl

**Explore** Who is the tallest in your class?

# Length words

Draw.

deeper

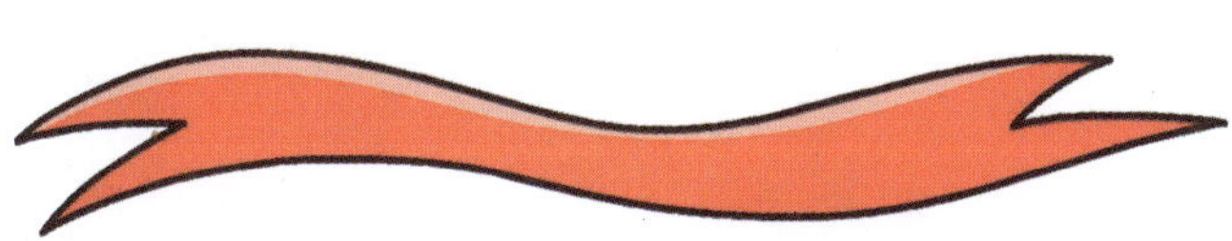

thicker

thinner

wider

# Comparing lengths

Draw your pencil.

Circle ◯ things **shorter** than your pencil.

Tick ✓ things that are **longer**.

## Mastery Checklist

I can:

- ☐ combine two or more groups of objects.
- ☐ use diagrams to help with combining quantities.
- ☐ count by ones to find the total.
- ☐ use comparing words to describe length.

# Problem solving

## Heights

In your class who is taller than you?
Who is shorter than you? Draw and write.

taller

You

shorter

**Challenge!**
Who is the same height as you?

I can solve a problem by:

☐ comparing heights. ☐ acting it out and drawing picture.

# Take away

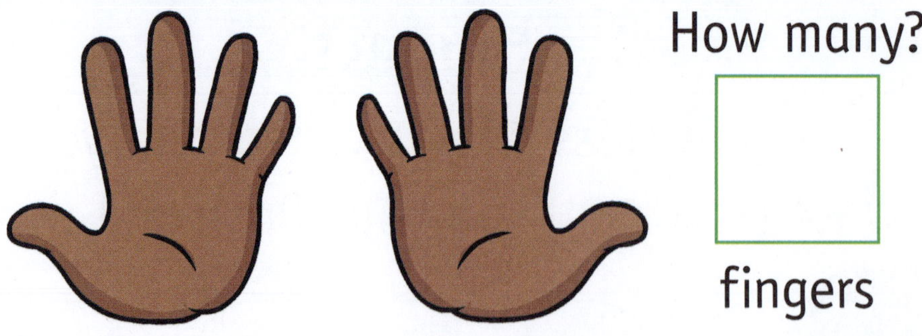

How many?

fingers

Take away 2.

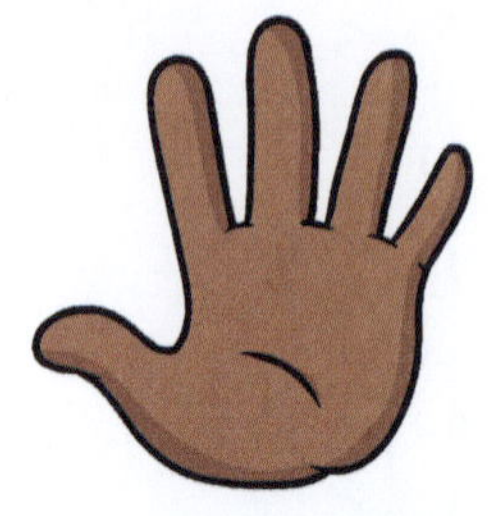

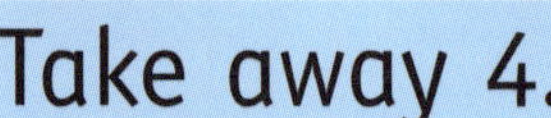
Take away 4.

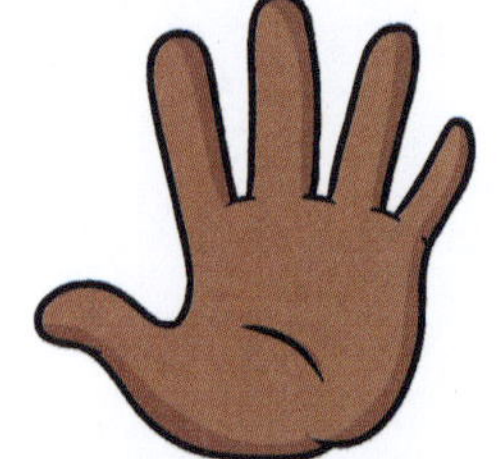
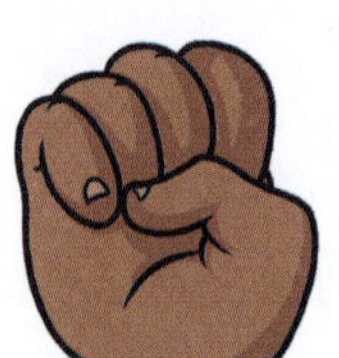

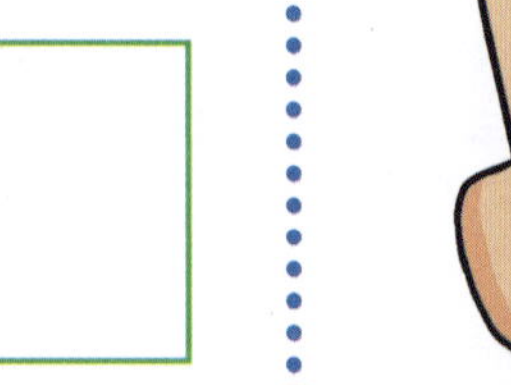

Take away 5.

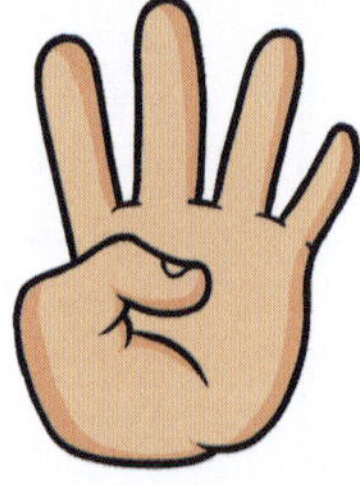

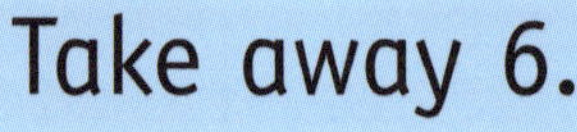
Take away 6.

Take away 7.

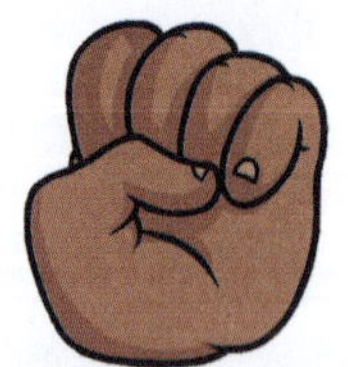

Take away 10.

Match.

5 take away 2 | 6 take away 4 | 3 take away 3

3 |  0 | 2



**Number** • **AC9MFN02** recognise the number of objects within a collection • **AC9MFN05** represent practical situations involving addition, subtraction and quantification

# Take away

Take away 2.

5 → ☐

☐ → ☐

☐ → ☐

☐ → ☐

☐ → ☐

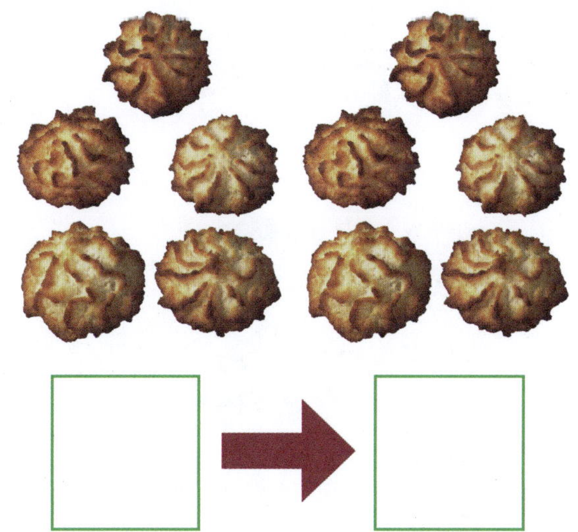

☐ → ☐

# Subtraction as cover up

How many? ☐

Cover up 2

How many left? ☐

How many? ☐

Cover up 3

How many left? ☐

How many? ☐

Cover up 6

How many left? ☐

How many? ☐

Cover up 4

How many left? ☐

How many? ☐

Cover up 5

How many left? ☐



**Number** • **AC9MFN05** represent practical situations involving addition, subtraction and quantification with physical and virtual materials and use counting or subitising strategies

# Counting back

Count back

1 2 3 4 5 6 7 8 9 10

Count back 1. 3 4

| | | | | | |
|---|---|---|---|---|---|
| 4 | ☐ | 7 | ☐ | 5 | ☐ |
| 3 | ☐ | 8 | ☐ | 10 | ☐ |

Count back 2. 4 5 6

| | | | | | |
|---|---|---|---|---|---|
| 6 | ☐ | 4 | ☐ | 8 | ☐ |
| 5 | ☐ | 2 | ☐ | 9 | ☐ |

Take away 1. ☐

Take away 2. ☐

## Mastery Checklist

I can:
- ☐ take away part of a group of objects to show subtraction.
- ☐ use fingers to solve subtraction questions.
- ☐ use diagrams to help with separating quantities.
- ☐ count by ones to find the difference.

# How old are we?

**Investigation 2**

Draw a face for each child in your class.

4 year olds

5 year olds

6 year olds

How many?

4 year olds

5 year olds 

6 year olds

# How old are we?

Investigation 2

How old are you? ____________

How many birthdays have you had? ____________

Draw a cake for each birthday.

Draw candles on each cake.

Write a number on each cake.

How many candles altogether? ____________

To do this, I needed to:

- ☐ collect data from my peers.
- ☐ make a data display.
- ☐ count forwards to 20.

I enjoyed this task! ☆☆☆☆☆

# Revision

**1** Take away 1.

How many left? ☐

How many left? ☐

**2** Take away 2.

How many left? ☐

How many left? ☐

**3** How many? Match to a number.

15

12

9

# Revision

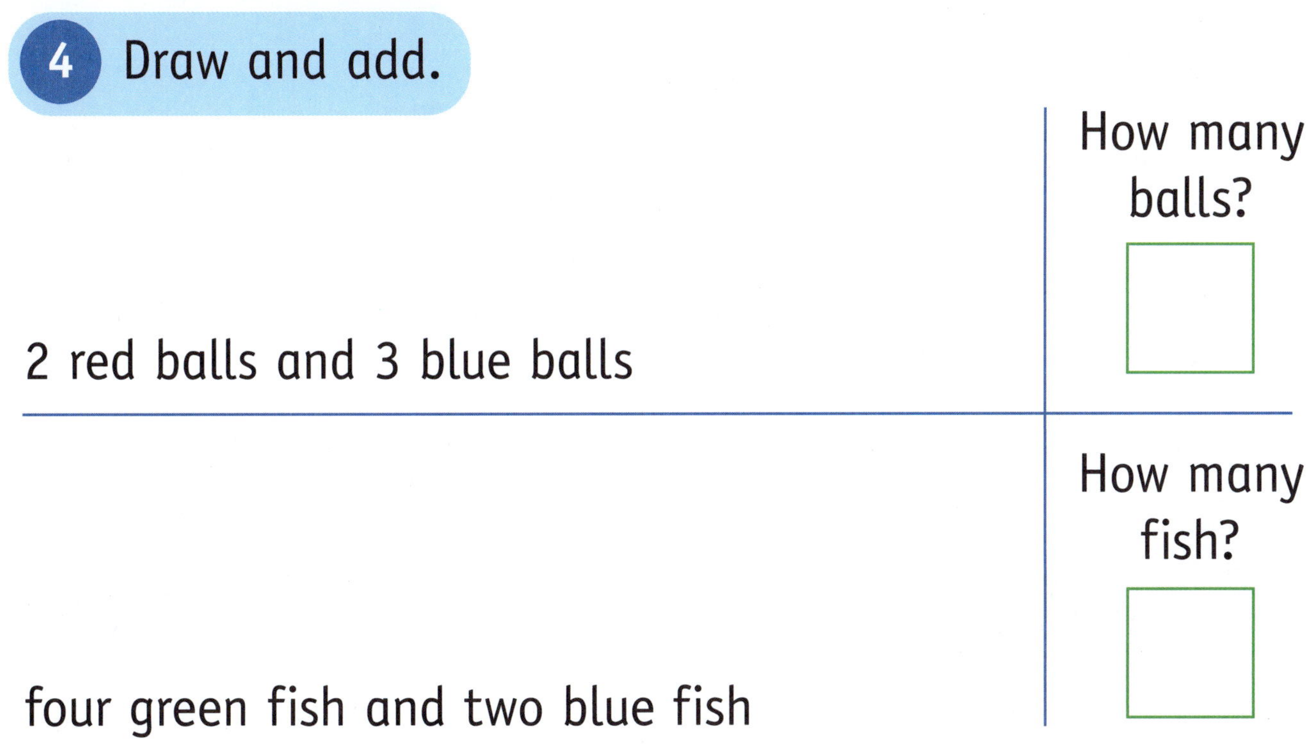

## 4 Draw and add.

2 red balls and 3 blue balls

How many balls?

four green fish and two blue fish

How many fish?

## 5 Write in order.

## 6 Circle:

the tallest.

the shortest.

# 3D objects

Match.

box shape

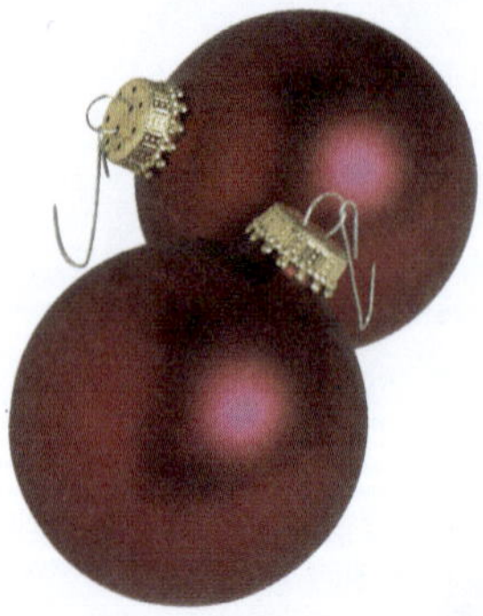

ball shape

# Objects that roll

Colour the things that roll.
Circle the things that stack.

How many roll? ☐ do not roll? ☐

How many stack? ☐ do not stack? ☐

# Ordering the days of the week

Draw lines to match. Write the missing days.

|  |  |
| --- | --- |
| Sunday |  |
| | |
| Tuesday | |
| | |
| Thursday |  |
| | |
| Saturday |  |
| | |
| Monday |  |
| |  |
| Wednesday |  |
| |  |

Monday

Friday

Wednesday

Thursday

Sunday

Tuesday

How many days were:

 **Measurement • AC9MFM02** sequence days of the week and times of the day including morning, lunchtime, afternoon and night time, and connect them to familiar events and actions

# O'clock

Write the numbers. Draw the hour hand for your favourite time.

**o'clock = Big hand is on 12.**

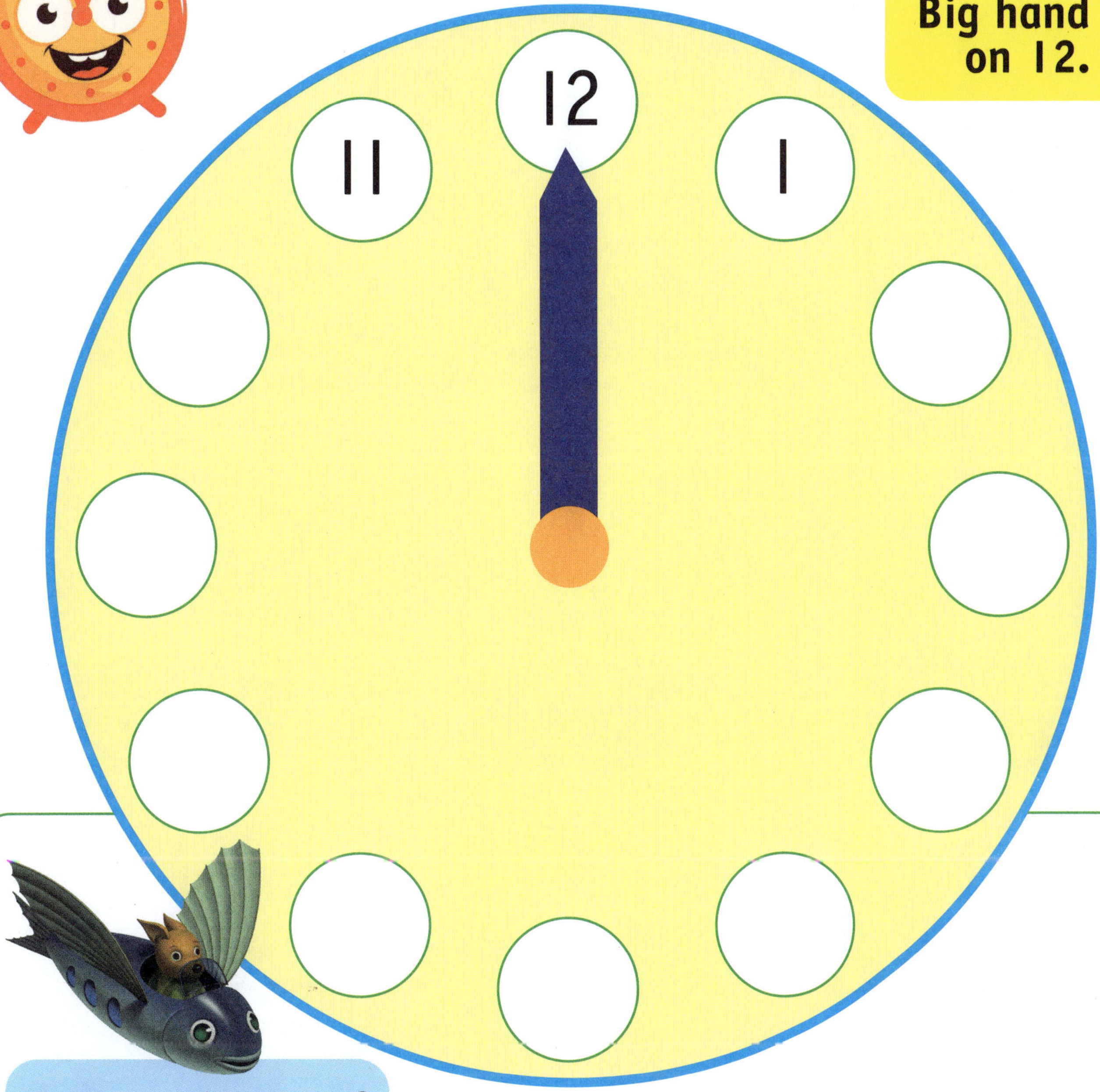

12

11

1

Draw a picture of you at this time.

# O'clock times

**o'clock =**
**Little hand is on the hour.**
**Big hand is on 12.**

Draw the hour hand.

3 o'clock

6 o'clock

9 o'clock

2 o'clock

5 o'clock

10 o'clock

1 o'clock

4 o'clock

7 o'clock

## Mastery Checklist

I can:
- ☐ sort objects and identify how I sorted them.
- ☐ identify if 3D objects will stack or roll.
- ☐ name and order the days of the week.
- ☐ make an analogue clock.

# Shape patterns

Draw the next two shapes.

**Challenge!** This is a 2 pattern.
Describe each of the patterns.
Write the number.

2 2

# Number patterns

Continue the pattern.

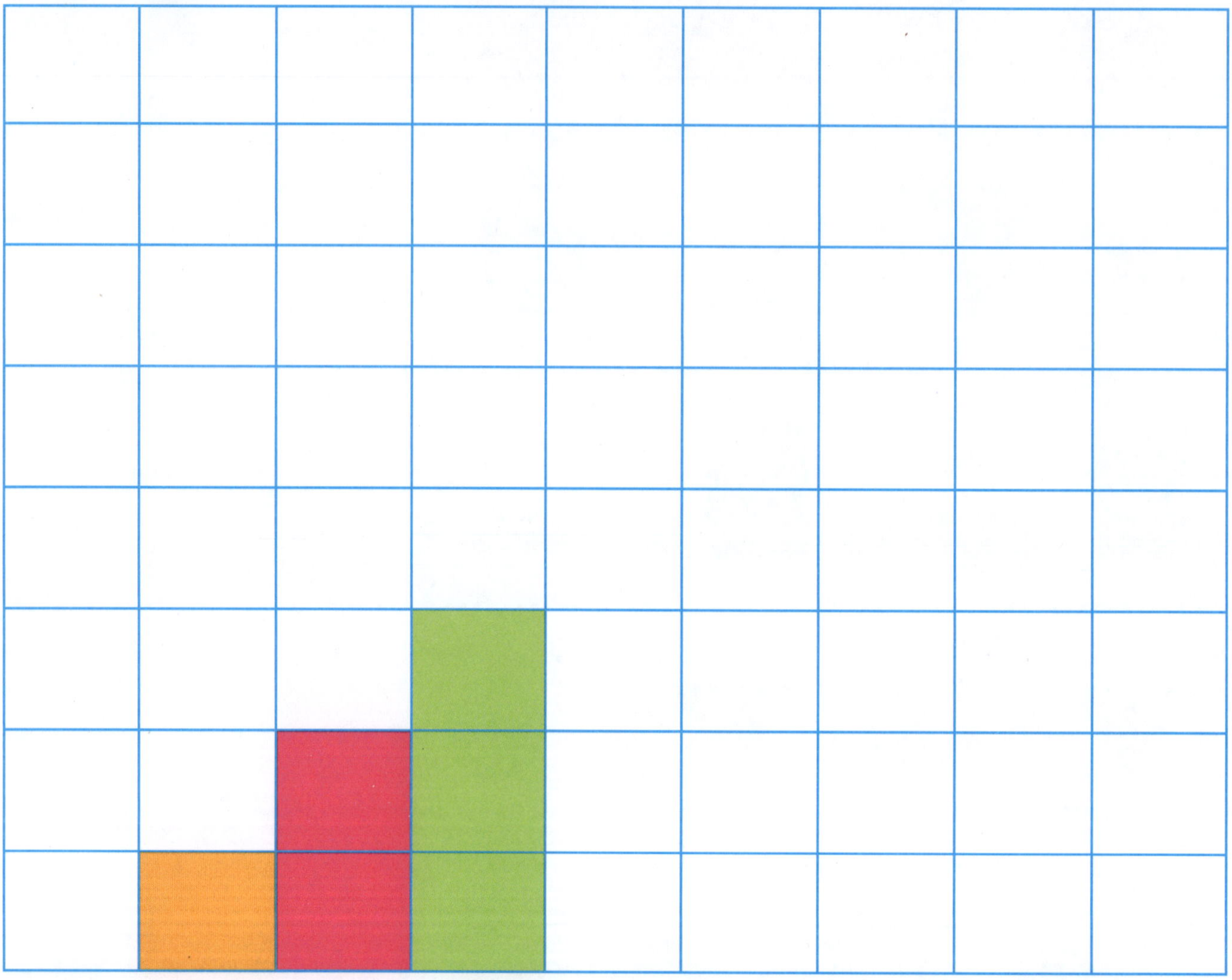

| 0 | 1 | 2 | 3 | | | | | |
|---|---|---|---|---|---|---|---|---|

The pattern is add ☐ .

Write your own number pattern.

☐ ☐ ☐ ☐ ☐ ☐ ☐

 **Number • AC9MFN05** represent practical situations involving addition, subtraction and quantification with physical and virtual materials and use counting or subitising strategies

# Patterns

Complete the shape patterns.
Write a number pattern to match.

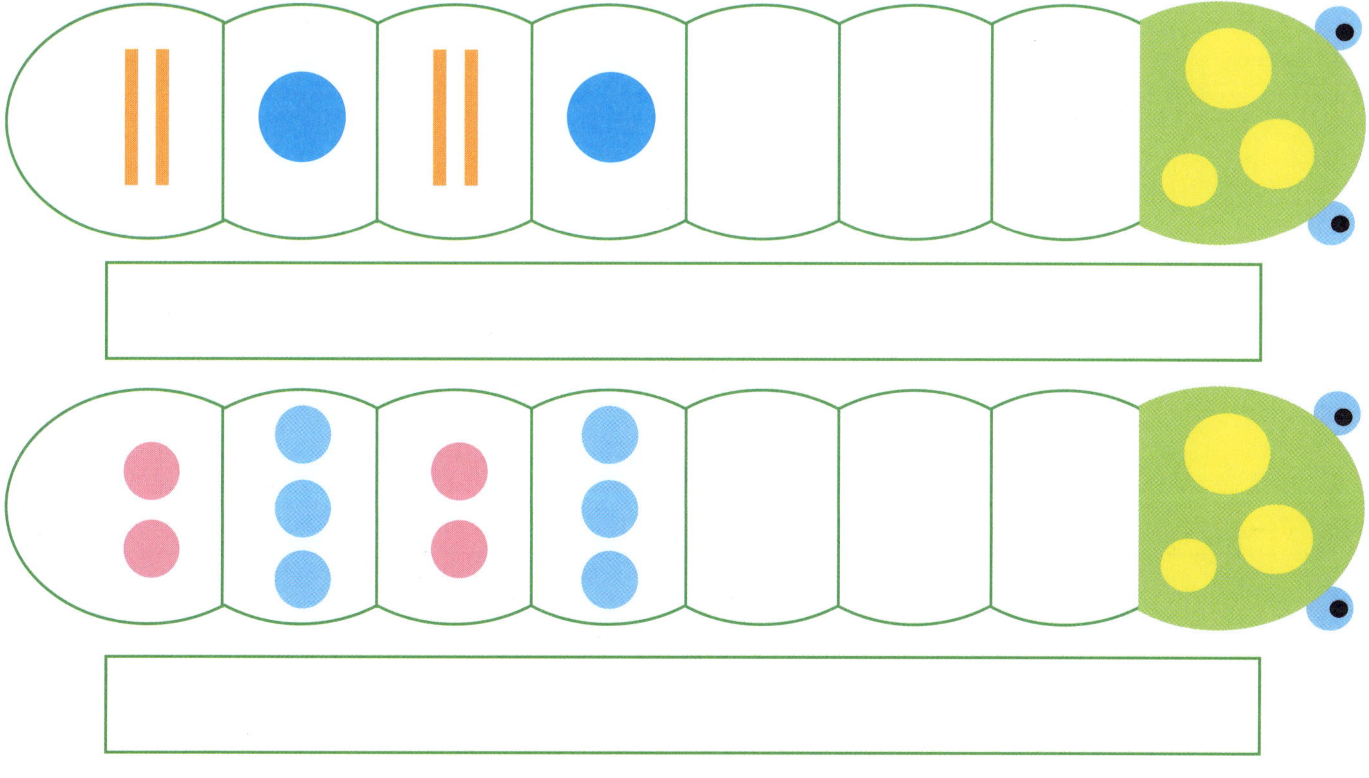

Draw your own pattern.

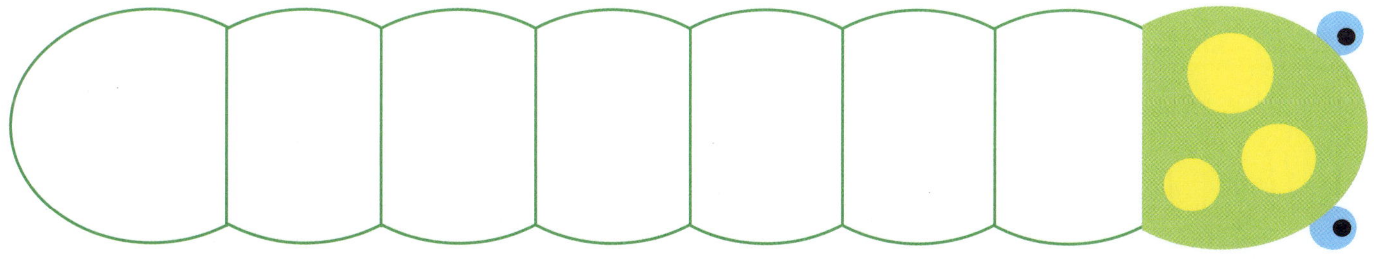

Colour squares **red** and triangles **green**.

Change each square to a circle. Draw the new pattern.

# Problem solving

## Patterns

Use colour to make a pattern.

Write about your pattern.

Use colour to make another pattern on the number chart.

| | | | | | | | | | |
|---|---|---|---|---|---|---|---|---|---|
| 1 | 2 | 3 | 4 | 5 | 6 | 7 | 8 | 9 | 10 |
| 11 | 12 | 13 | 14 | 15 | 16 | 17 | 18 | 19 | 20 |
| 21 | 22 | 23 | 24 | 25 | 26 | 27 | 28 | 29 | 30 |

Write about your pattern.

I can solve a problem by:

☐ making patterns using colour. ☐ using a diagram.

# Above, below and inside

Draw the toy that is:

above

above

below

Colour the shirts of the children **inside** the sandpit.

# Position

Draw something.

between

on top

inside

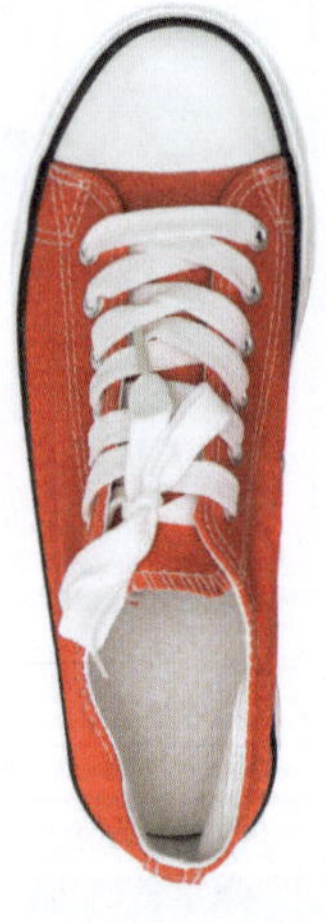

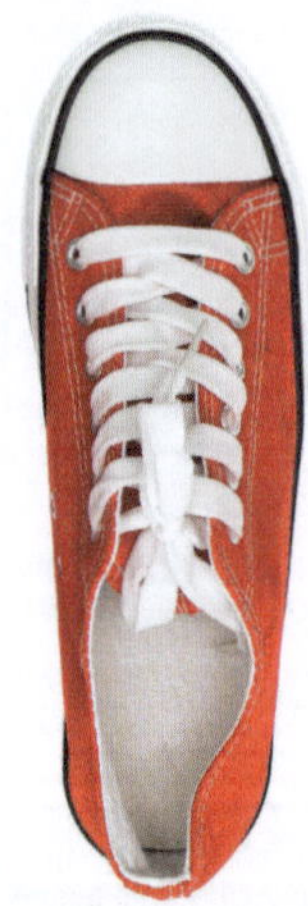

left

right

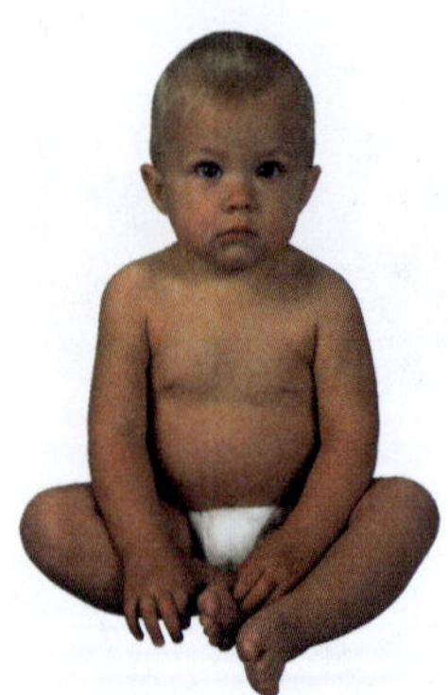

beside

under

in front of

behind



**Space • AC9MFSP02** describe the position and location of themselves and objects in relation to other people and objects within a familiar space

# Position

Use the wordbank to complete.

**Wordbank**
- on
- over
- far
- under
- above
- up
- near

The pine trees are ________________ away.

The boat is ________________ the water.

The car is ________________ the dog.

The car is ________________ the road.

The dog is ________________ the box and ________________ the tree.

## Mastery Checklist

I can:
- ☐ make repeating patterns using shapes and numbers.
- ☐ follow simple directions to position objects.
- ☐ describe the position of an object.

## Revision • Term 2

### 1 Add.

5 and 3 more

6 and 2 more

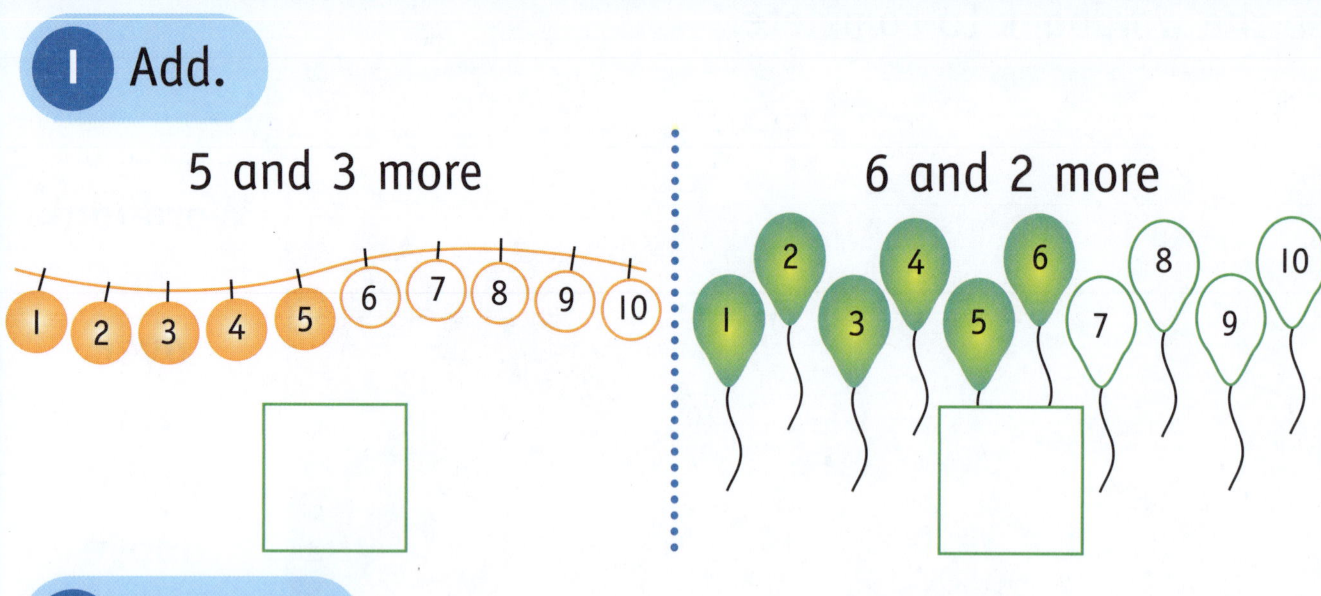


### 2 Make 10.

4 and ☐

2 and ☐

7 and ☐

1 and ☐

### 3 Draw a taller girl in front. Draw a shorter boy behind.

## 4 What time is it?

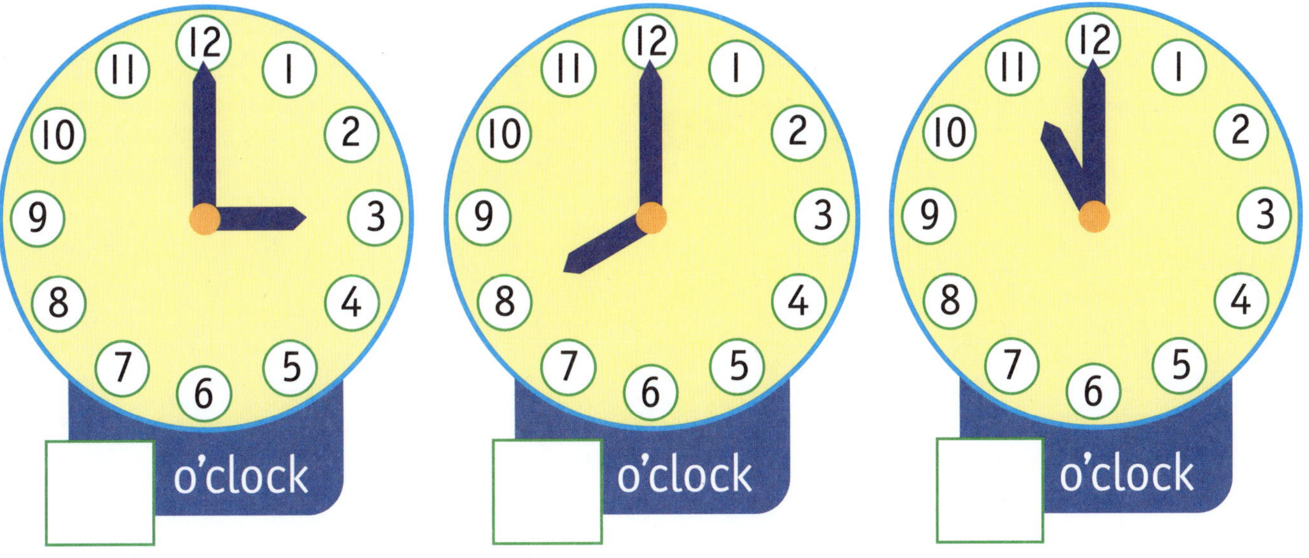


## 5 Draw and colour the next two shapes.

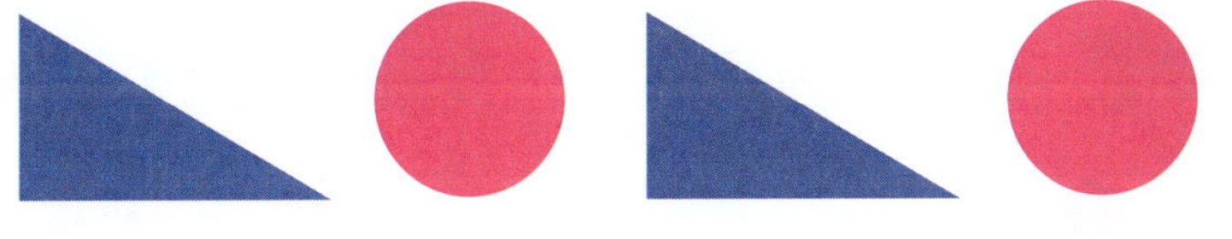

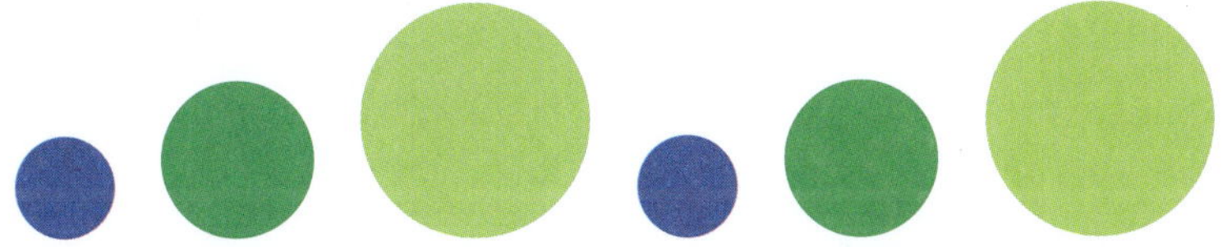

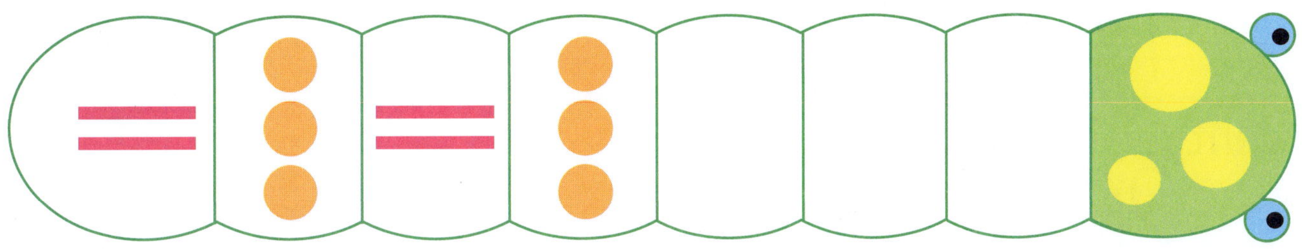

# Number names to 20

| | | |
|---|---|---|
| eleven | 11 | |
| twelve | 12 | |
| thirteen | 13 | |
| fourteen | 14 | |
| fifteen | 15 | |
| sixteen | 16 | |
| seventeen | 17 | |
| eighteen | 18 | |
| nineteen | 19 | |
| twenty | 20 | |

| | |
|---|---|
| 14 | eighteen |
| 18 | fourteen |
| 15 | sixteen |
| 16 | twenty |
| 20 | nineteen |
| 19 | fifteen |

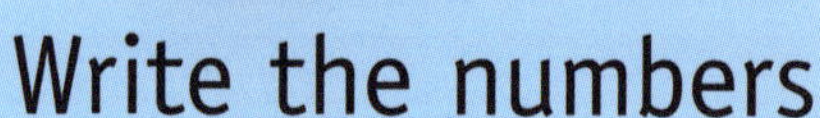

Draw dots.

| Write the numbers. | | Draw dots. |
|---|---|---|
| ten | ____ | ●●●●● ●●●●● |
| twenty | ____ | |
| twelve | ____ | |
| eleven | ____ | |



**Number • AC9MFN01** name, represent and order numbers including zero to at least 20, using physical and virtual materials and numerals

# Making groups to twenty

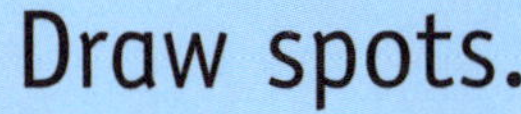

The spotty dog loves spots.

Draw spots.

11

14

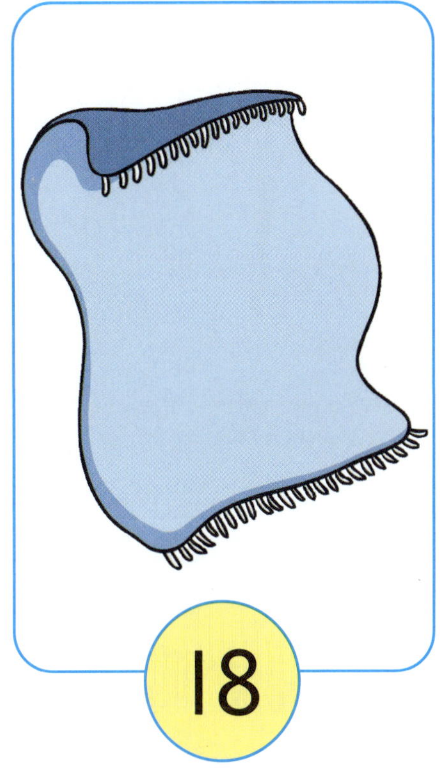

18

Colour the correct number.

12

15

20

# Comparing numbers to 20

1 How many? Tick ✓ the larger number.

2 Colour the **larger** number.

3 Colour the **smallest** number.

# Order numbers to 20

Write the numbers in order.

1

15 16 14

14

2

3

17 20 13

4

19 11 15

5 What number comes

| | | |
|---|---|---|
| after 10 | 14 | before 17 |
| after 13 | 11 | before 15 |
| after 18 | 16 | before 20 |
| after 15 | 19 | before 12 |

## Problem solving

# On the farm

The farmer can see 5 heads and 12 legs.

What animals can the farmer see? Draw them.

I can solve a problem by:

☐ comparing groups and counting to 12. ☐ drawing a picture.



**Number • AC9MFN01** name, represent and order numbers to at least 20 • **AC9MFN03** quantify and compare collections to at least 20

# Counting to thirty

How many?

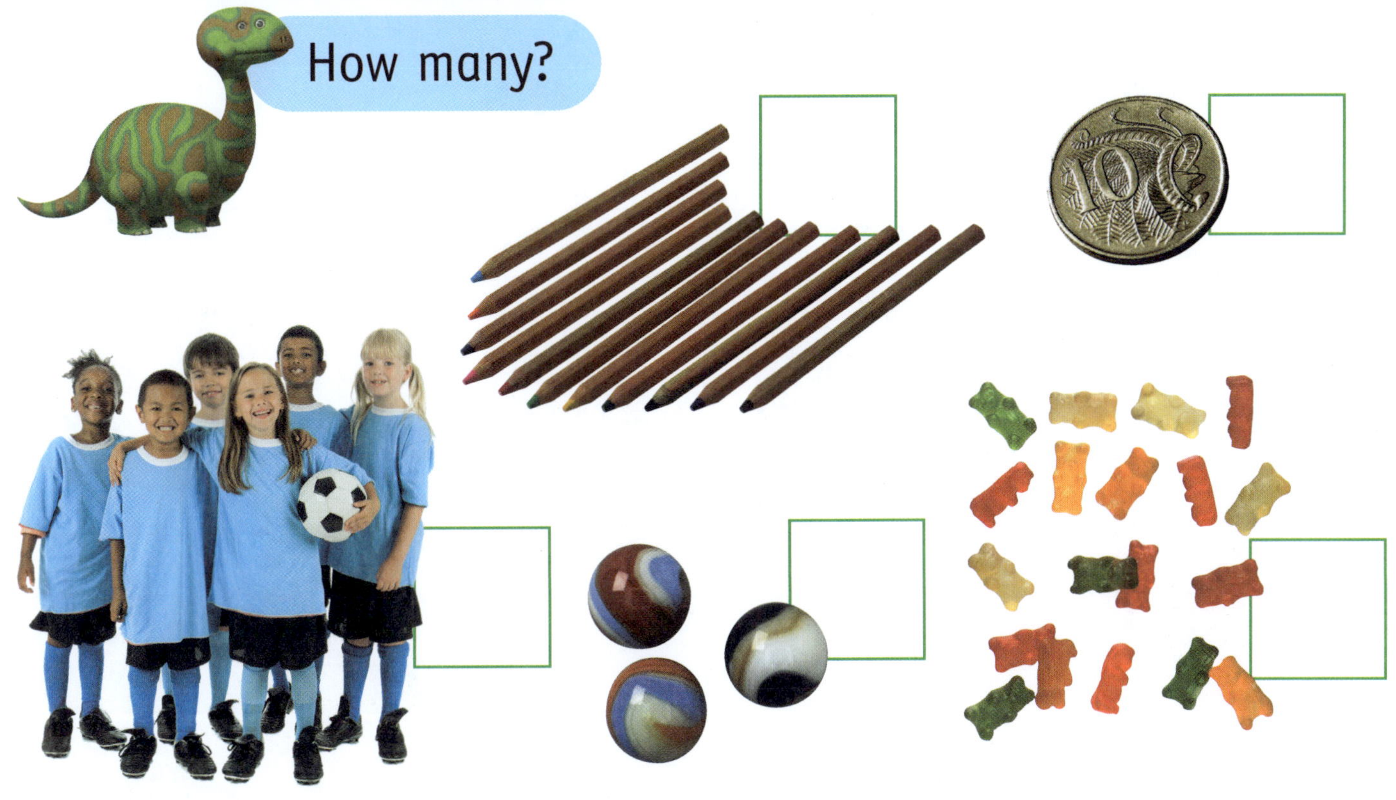

| 0 | 1 | 2 | 3 | 4 | 5 | 6 | 7 | 8 | 9 |
|---|---|---|---|---|---|---|---|---|---|
| 10 | 11 | 12 | 13 | 13 | 15 | 16 | 17 | 18 | 19 |
| 20 | 21 | 22 | 23 | 24 | 25 | 26 | 27 | 28 | 29 |
| 30 | | | | | | | | | |

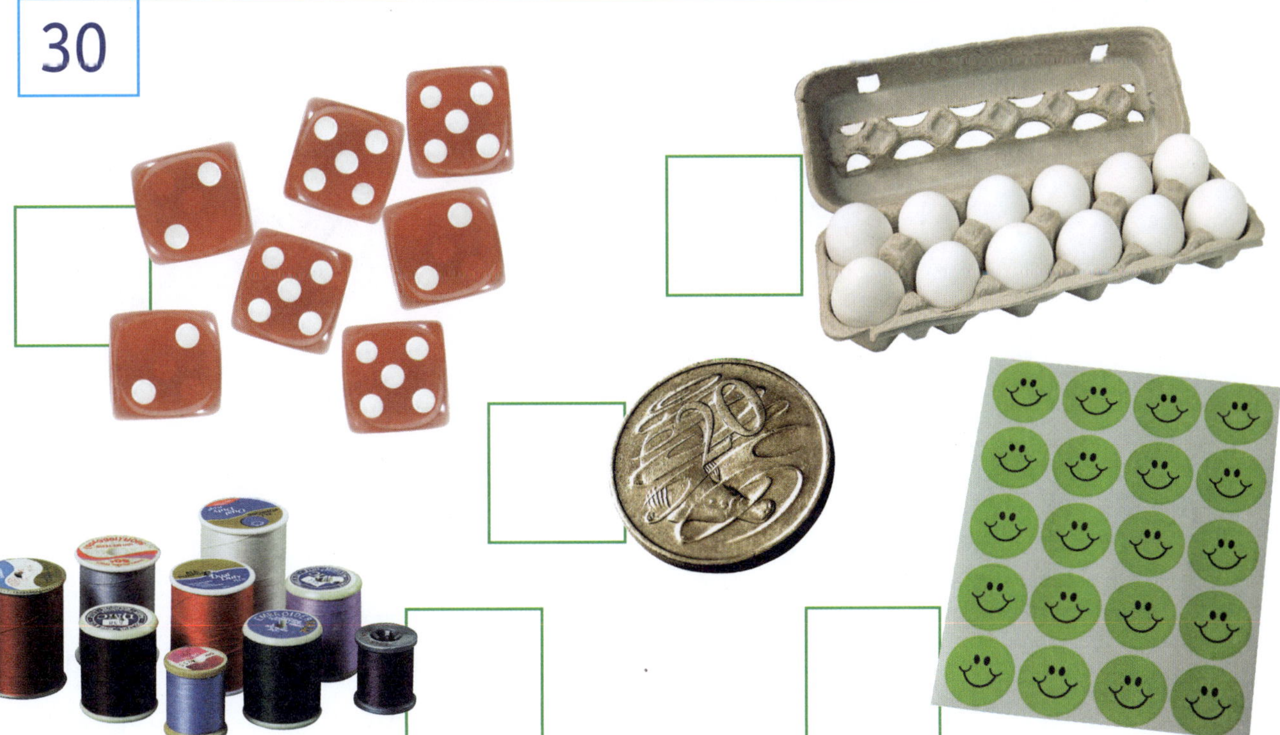

# Coins to 30c

Circle the coins to buy.

**Challenge!**

Choose 2. How much to buy both?

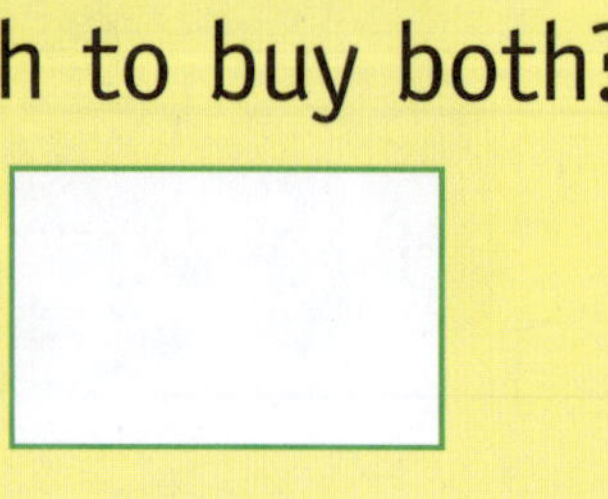

## Mastery Checklist

I can:

- [ ] count out a number of objects to 20.
- [ ] compare and order numbers to 20.
- [ ] identify the number after or before a number.
- [ ] count the total number in a group to 30.

# Problem solving

## 30 cents

You have 30 cents.
What coins could you have?
Show 4 different answers.

**Use real coins to try out different answers.**

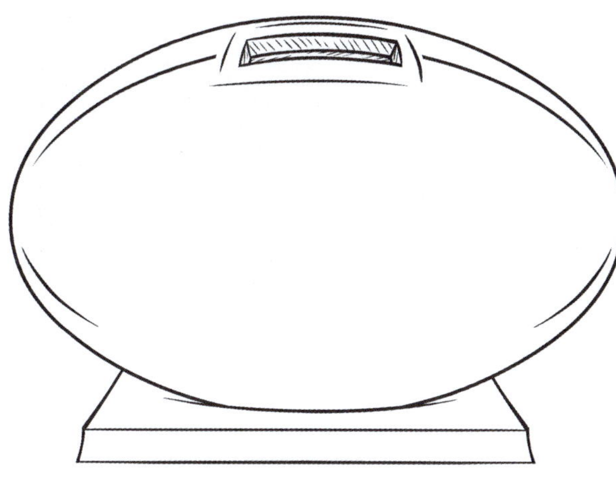

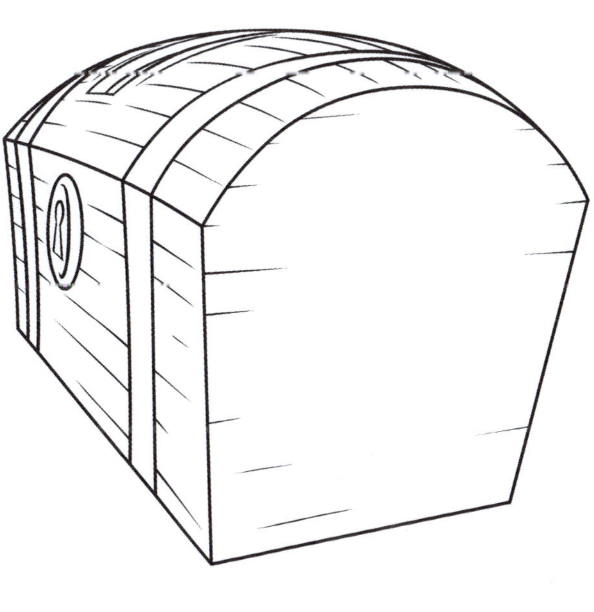

I can solve a problem by:

☐ adding coins to make 30. ☐ acting it out.

# Area

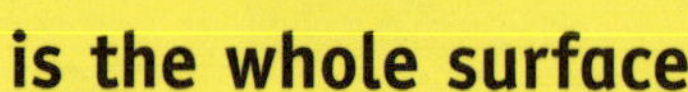

**Area** is the whole surface.

Circle the largest.

Colour the smallest and the largest.

Cover each butterfly with counters. How many?

# Measuring area

How many blocks cover each leaf?

cover to measure **area** in blocks

O smallest X biggest

# Comparing areas

Colour the **smallest** shape yellow and the **biggest** shape red. Colour the shape that is the **same size** blue.

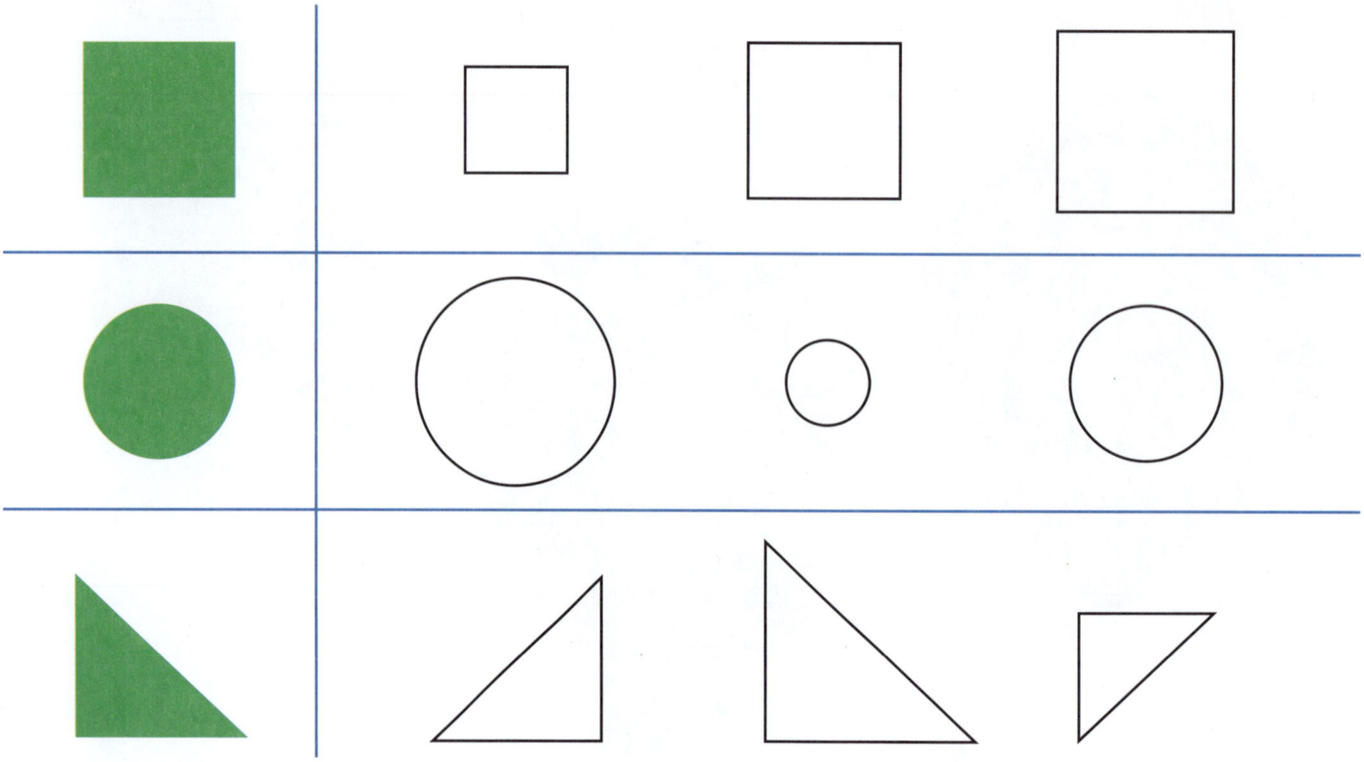

Circle the shape that is biggest.

Tick the shapes that are the same size.

# 2D shape pictures

Colour the shapes you can see.

How many?

| | |
|---|---|
| | squares |
| | circles |
| | triangles |
| | rectangles |

# Drawing shape patterns

Trace the shapes and continue the pattern. Colour each pattern.

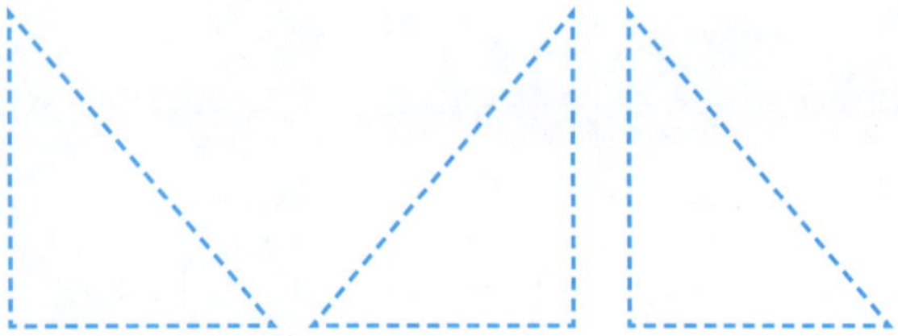

My shape pattern.

## Mastery Checklist

I can:
- ☐ use comparing words to describe areas.
- ☐ compare areas of two shapes.
- ☐ identify familiar shapes.
- ☐ make repeating patterns using shapes.

## Problem solving

# Shape sort

Find 2 shapes to go in each box.

| curved lines | straight lines |
| --- | --- |
| **3 corners** | **4 corners** |

I can solve a problem by:

☐ identifying features of shapes. ☐ drawing diagrams.

# Making groups

How many balls?

Circle groups

How many?

How many shells?

Circle groups

How many?



Number • AC9MFN06 represent practical situations involving equal sharing and grouping with physical and virtual materials and use counting or subitising strategies

# Making groups

Group 

How many fish?

How many?

Draw the two groups.

Red fish

Blue fish

# Recognising unequal groups

Cross out the different group.

Draw groups of 3.

Draw groups of 4.

# Groups of two and three

## Circle groups of 2.

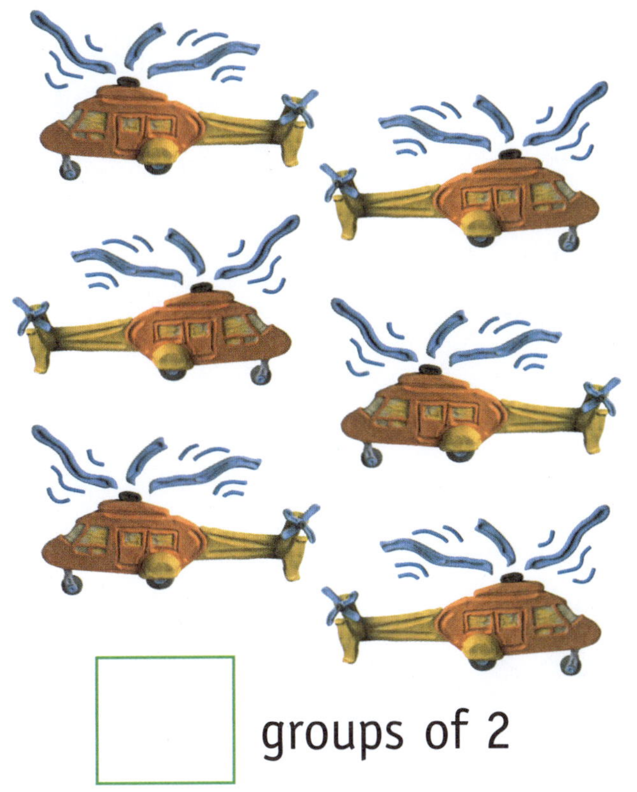

☐ groups of 2

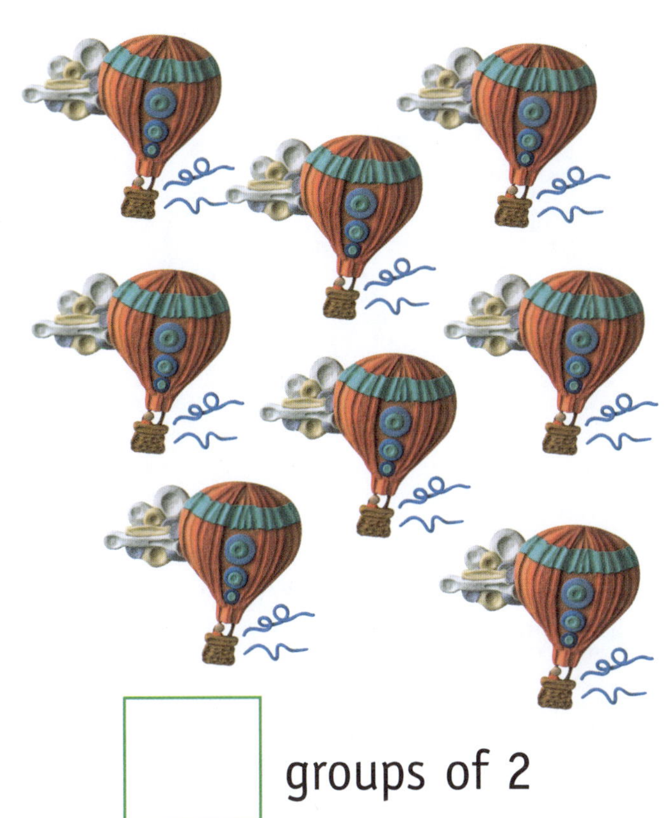

☐ groups of 2

## Circle groups of 3.

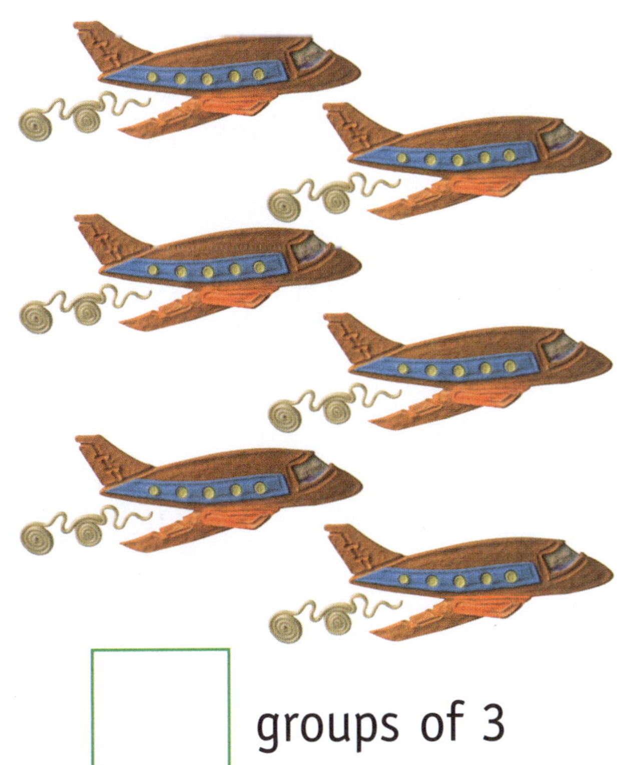

☐ groups of 3

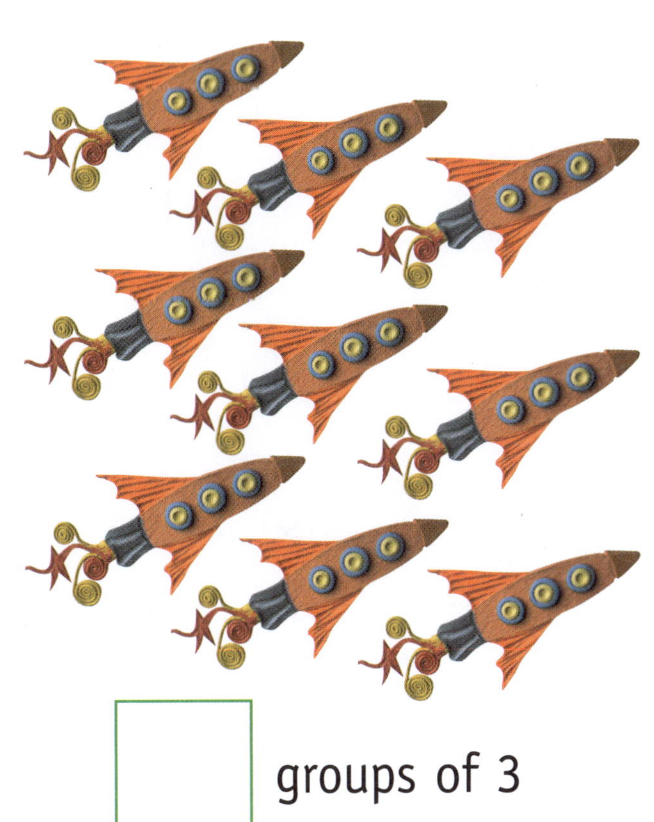

☐ groups of 3

# Equal groups

How many groups of two?

How many groups of three?

Make 3. Make 4. Make 2.

How many?

## Mastery Checklist

I can:

- [ ] label the number of objects in a group.
- [ ] identify if the number in each group is equal or not.
- [ ] record grouping and sharing using drawings, words and numerals.
- [ ] share a group of objects into smaller groups.

# Problem solving

## 2 fishing boats

Each child catches 2 fish.

How many fish do they catch? ☐

I can solve a problem by:

☐ adding groups together. ☐ counting by twos.

# Paper pets

Investigation 3

Make a paper pet out of shapes. Name your pet.

You can make more than one.

Glue or draw your pet here.

List the shapes in your pet.

**Space • AC9MFSP01** sort, name and create familiar shapes; recognise and describe familiar shapes within objects in the environment, giving reasons

# Paper pets

Investigation 3

Make a shape house for your shape pet.

Glue or draw your pet's house here.

List the shapes in your pet's house.

To do this, I needed to:

- ☐ move shapes around.
- ☐ make pictures using shapes.
- ☐ identify familiar shapes.

I enjoyed this task!

☆☆☆☆☆

# Revision

**1** Write the missing numbers.

| | | | | | | | | | |
|---|---|---|---|---|---|---|---|---|---|
| | 2 | 3 | | 5 | | 7 | | | 10 |
| 11 | 12 | | 14 | 15 | 16 | | 18 | | 20 |
| 21 | | | 24 | | 26 | 27 | 28 | 29 | 30 |

**2** How many?

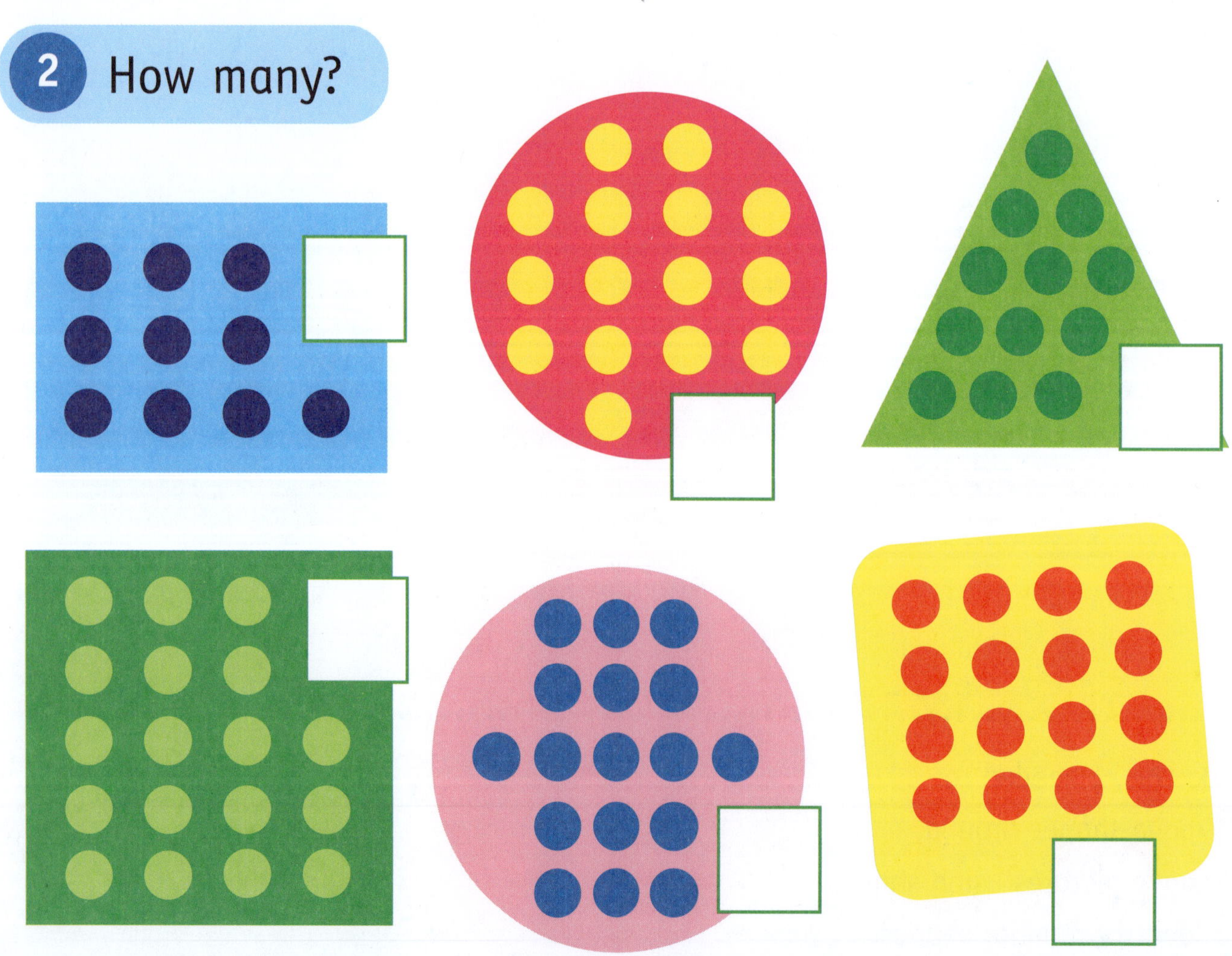

# Revision

3 Match.

inside

outside

4 Match.

triangle | square | circle | rectangle

5 Colour the shirts that are the same size.

# Addition to ten

Cover each circle with a counter. How many? ☐

Make 10 using two colours.

☐ and ☐

☐ and ☐

☐ and ☐

☐ and ☐

☐ and ☐

☐ and ☐

Now use three colours.

☐ and ☐ and ☐

☐ and ☐ and ☐

# Counting with money

Circle the correct money.

$7 — $5 $1 $1 $1 $1 $1 — $5 + ☐ = $7

$9 — $5 $1 $1 $1 $1 $1 — $5 + ☐ = $9

$6 — $5 $1 $1 $1 $1 $1 — $5 + ☐ = $6

$10 — $5 $1 $1 $1 $1 $1 — $5 + ☐ = $10

How much altogether?

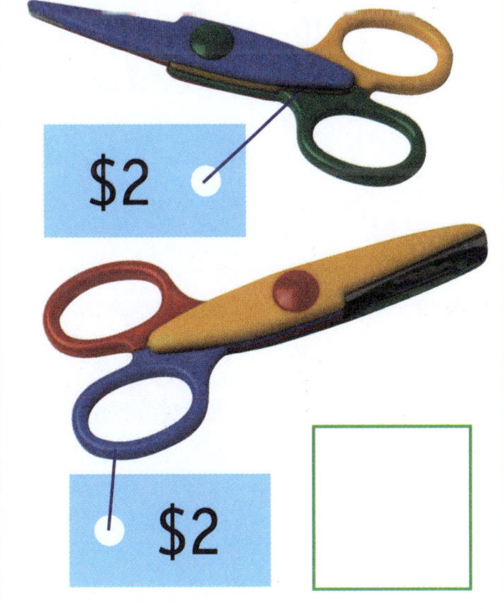


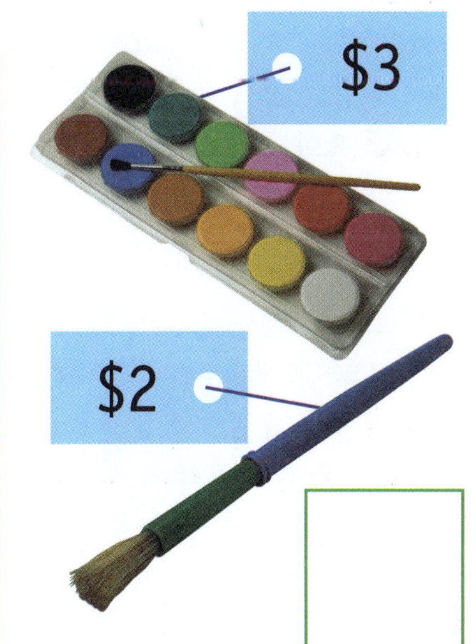

# Adding three numbers

How many dots? Write numbers and add.

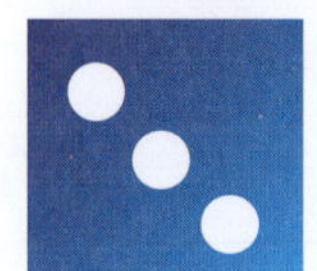  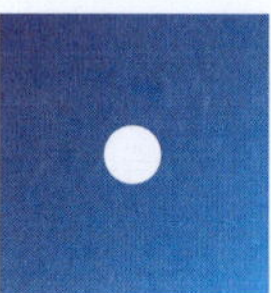

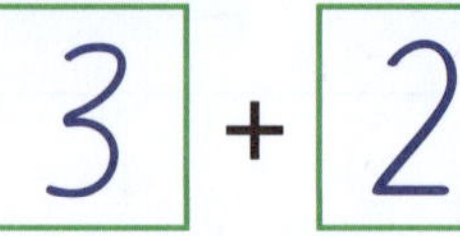

3 + 2 + 1 = ☐

 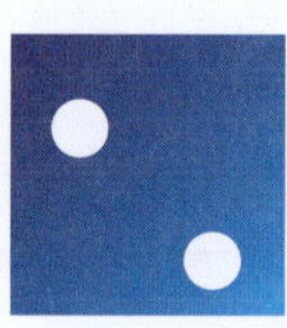 

☐ + ☐ + ☐ = ☐

 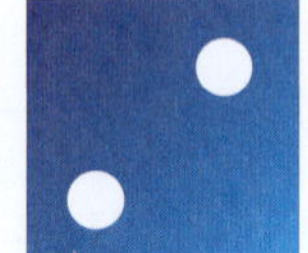 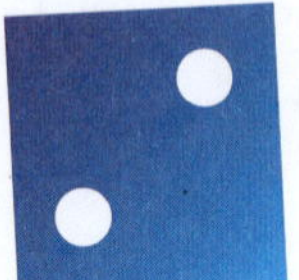

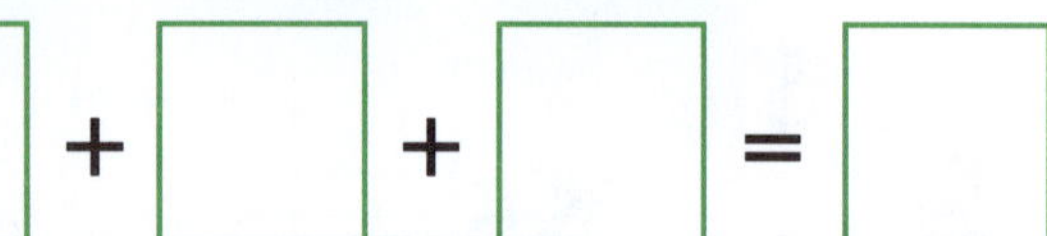

☐ + ☐ + ☐ = ☐

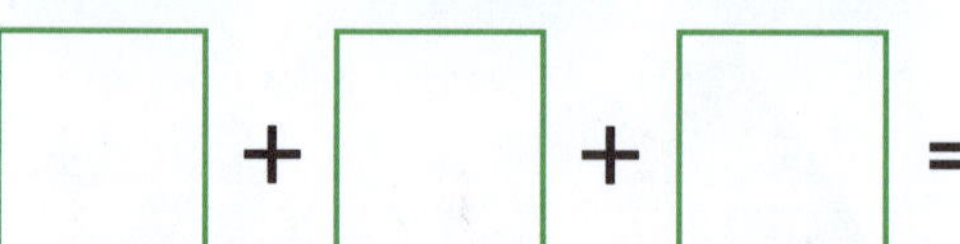

☐ + ☐ + ☐ = ☐

Colour to add.

3 + 2 + 1 = ☐

4 + 2 + 2 = ☐

1 2 3 4 5 6 7 8 9 10

3 + 3 + 1 = ☐

6 + 1 + 1 = ☐

1 2 3 4 5 6 7 8 9 10

5 + 2 + 1 = ☐

4 + 3 + 1 = ☐



**Number • AC9MFN02** recognise the number of objects within a collection • AC9MFN05 represent practical situations involving addition, subtraction and quantification

# A dozen

3 numbers add to 12. What could the numbers be?

I can solve a problem by:

☐ adding three numbers. ☐ writing number sentences.

# The seasons

Draw a picture for each season.

December
January
February

March
April
May

Summer

Autumn

Spring

Winter

September
October
November

June
July
August

Cross out the wrong word.

Summer comes before / after Spring.

Winter comes before / after Autumn.

# O'clock times

## What time is it?

☐ o'clock ☐ o'clock ☐ o'clock

☐ o'clock ☐ o'clock ☐ o'clock

☐ o'clock ☐ o'clock ☐ o'clock

## Mastery Checklist

I can:

- ☐ find sets of numbers up to ten.
- ☐ use 10 to make numbers from 11 to 20.
- ☐ use diagrams to help with combining groups.
- ☐ read analogue clocks to the hour using the term 'o'clock'.

# Half a length

**Halves** are two equal parts.

Colour the ribbons that are cut in half.

Cut the strings in half.

# Halfway

Mark the halfway point. Colour one half.

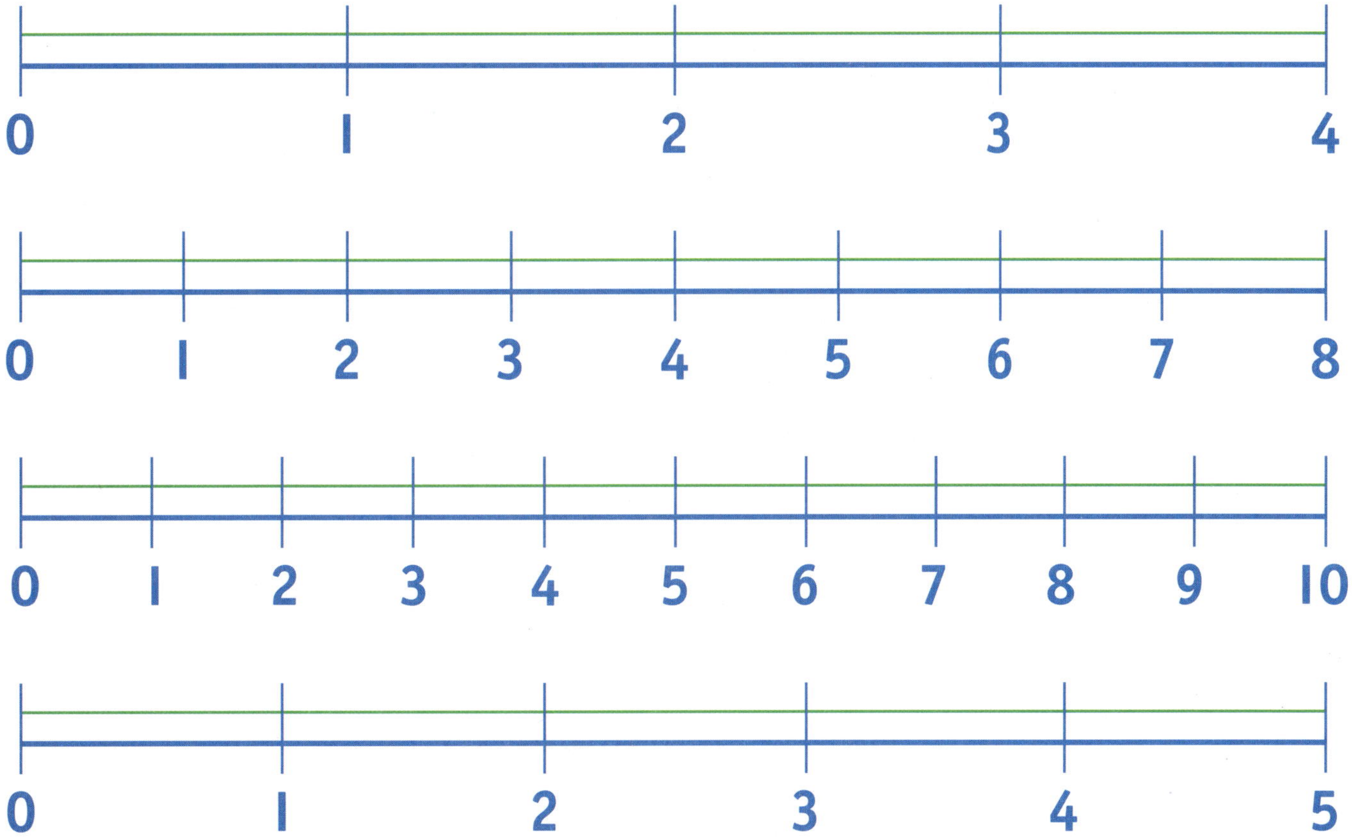

0 1 2 3 4

0 1 2 3 4 5 6 7 8

0 1 2 3 4 5 6 7 8 9 10

0 1 2 3 4 5

Draw a dog about halfway along the path.
Draw a boy less than halfway along the path.
Draw a girl more than halfway along the path.

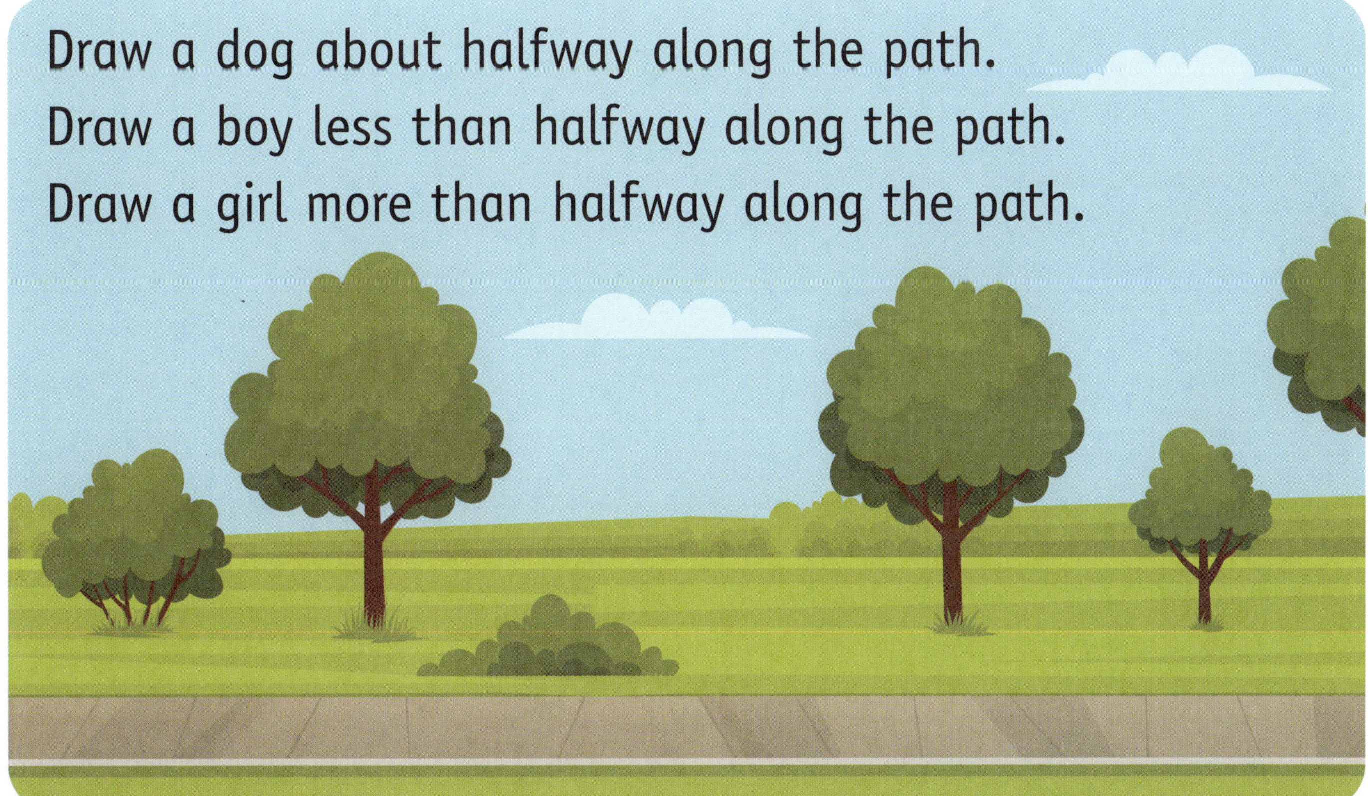

# Sorting 2D shapes

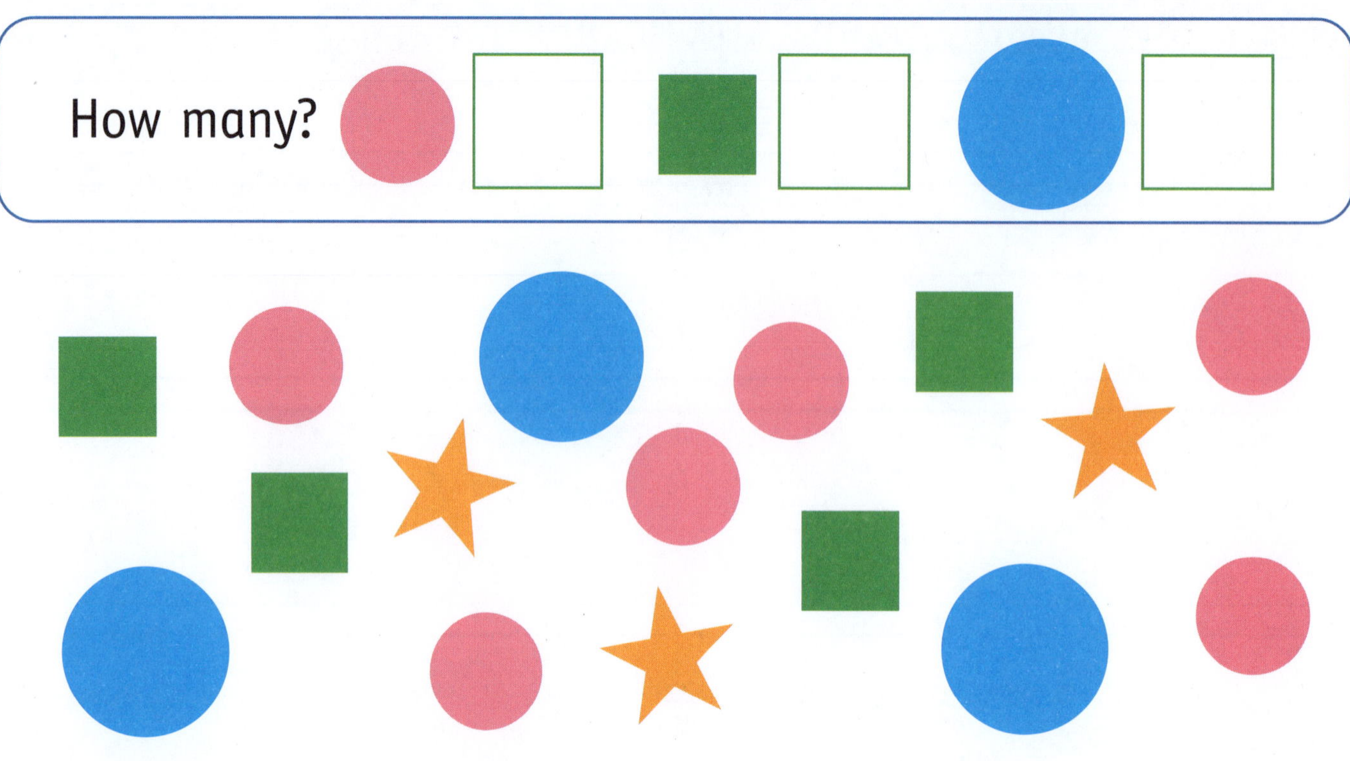


Draw each shape in the picture graph.

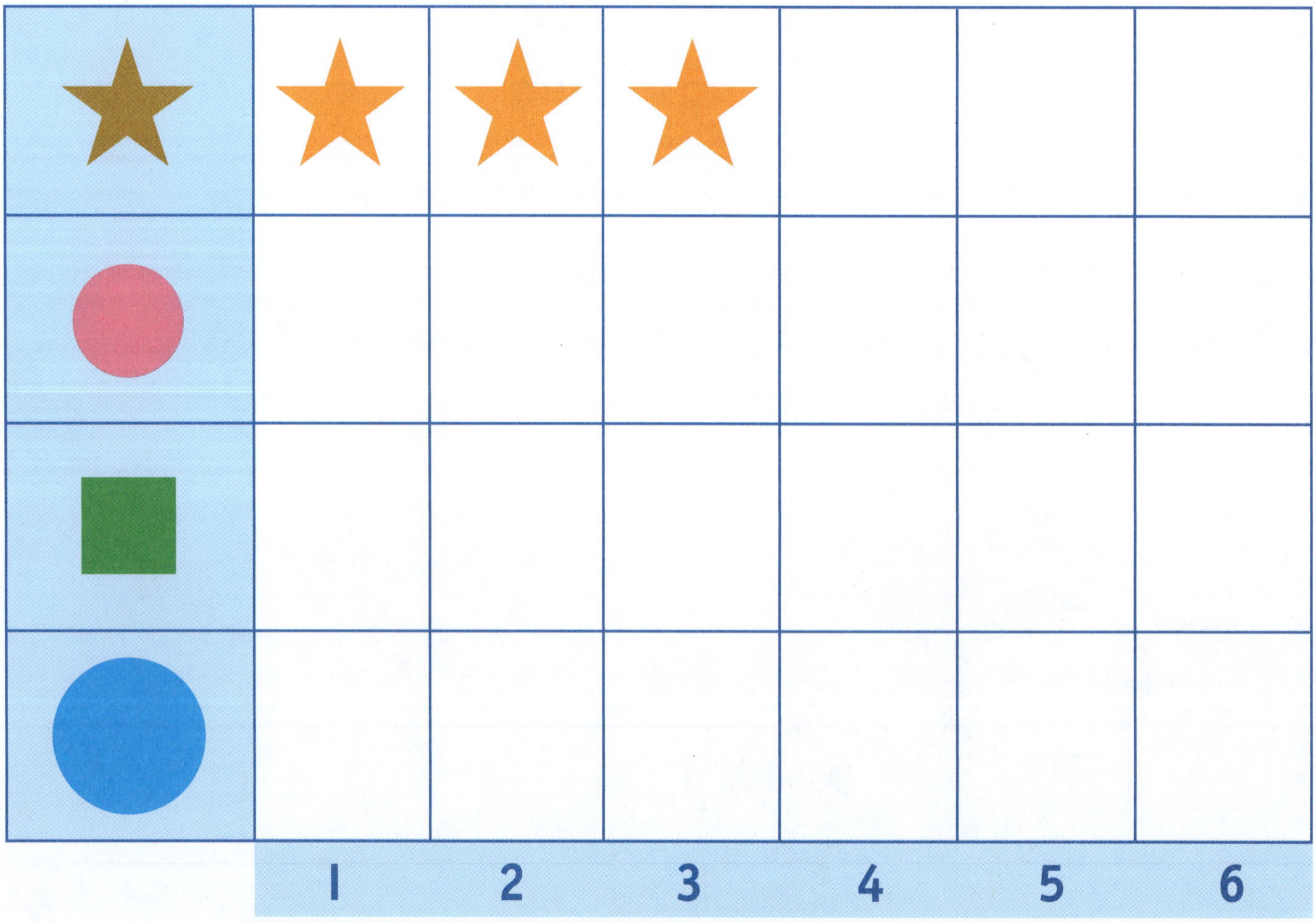

| | | | | | | |
|---|---|---|---|---|---|---|
| | | | | | | |
| | | | | | | |
| | | | | | | |
| | | | | | | |
| | 1 | 2 | 3 | 4 | 5 | 6 |

# Weather

Complete your own weather chart.

| Monday | Tuesday | Wednesday | Thursday | Friday |
|---|---|---|---|---|
| | | | | |
| Monday | Tuesday | Wednesday | Thursday | Friday |
| | | | | |

Colour one square for each day.

I square = I day

How many days?

## Mastery Checklist

I can:
- [ ] cut a length into two equal parts.
- [ ] identify positions as 'about', 'more than' or 'less than' halfway.
- [ ] collect data and form a data display.
- [ ] compare the sizes of groups by counting.

# Revision • Term 3

**1** Colour one half of each length.

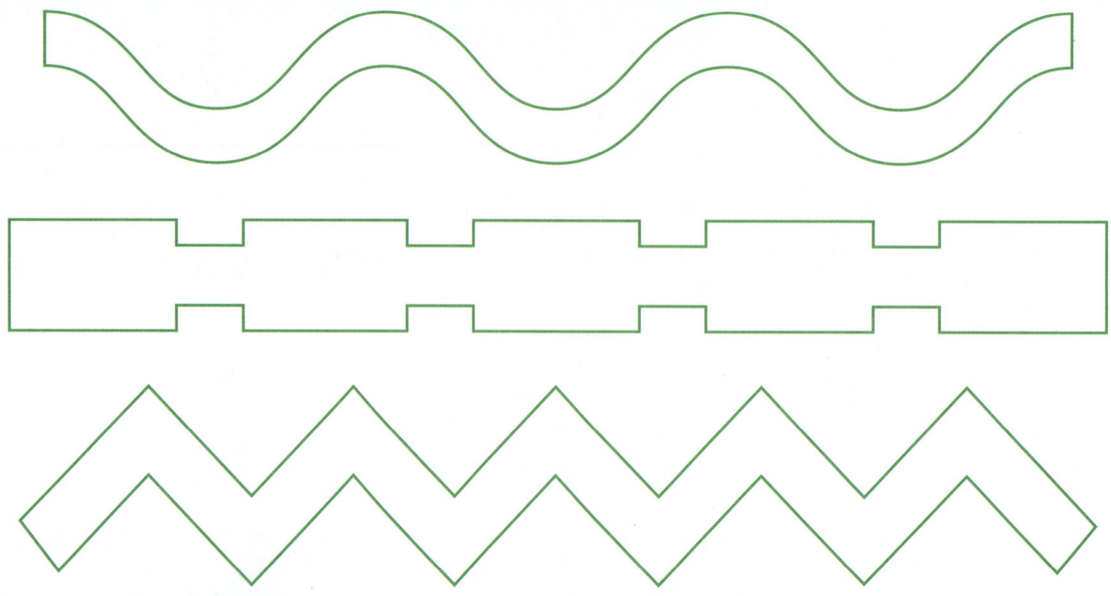

**2** Draw the other half. Name the shape.

## 3 Write the missing numbers.

| 12 | 13 | 14 | | | |
|---|---|---|---|---|---|
| 20 | | 18 | 17 | | |

## 4 Add.

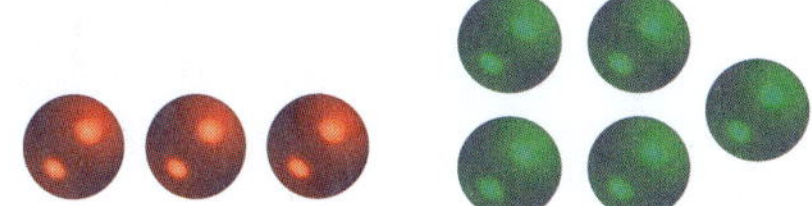

3 + 5 = □

□ + □ = □

## 5 How much?

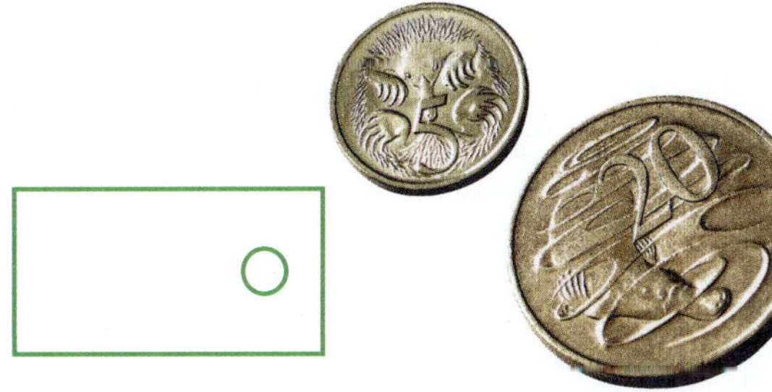

## 6 Change blue to yellow. Colour the new pattern.

# First to fifth

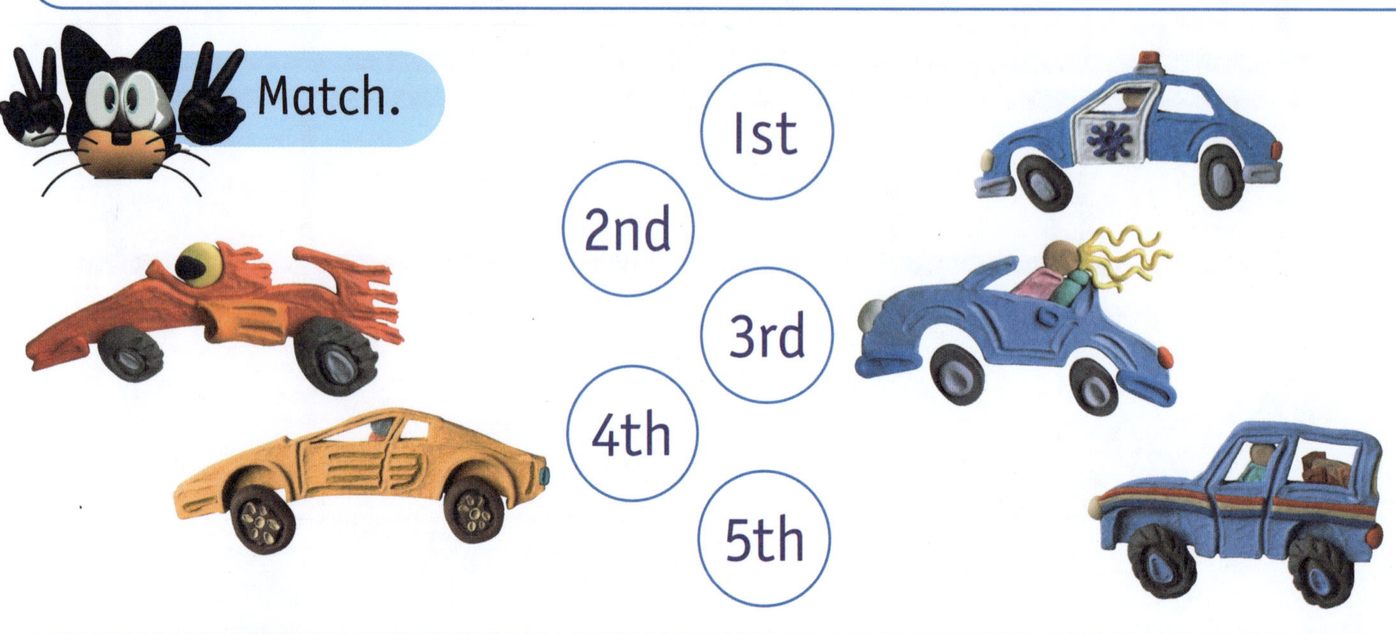


Colour.

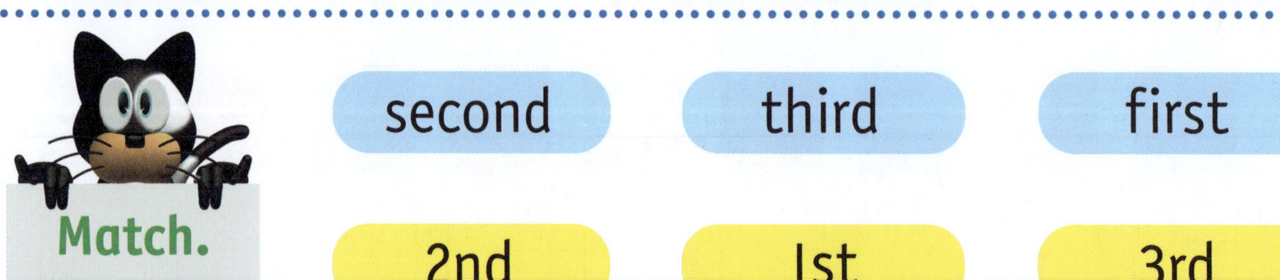




**Number • AC9MFN01** name, represent and order numbers including zero to at least 20, using physical and virtual materials and numerals

# Ordinal numbers to tenth



| 6th | 7th | 8th | 9th | 10th |
|---|---|---|---|---|
| sixth | seventh | eighth | ninth | tenth |

Match.

6th

7th

8th

9th

10th

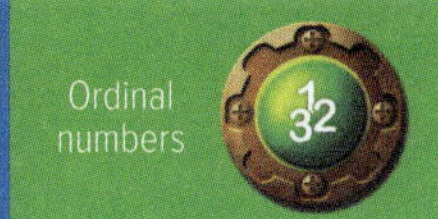

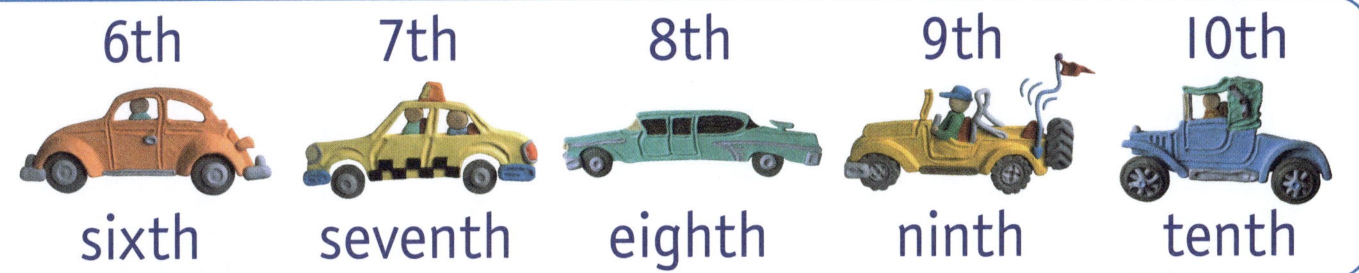

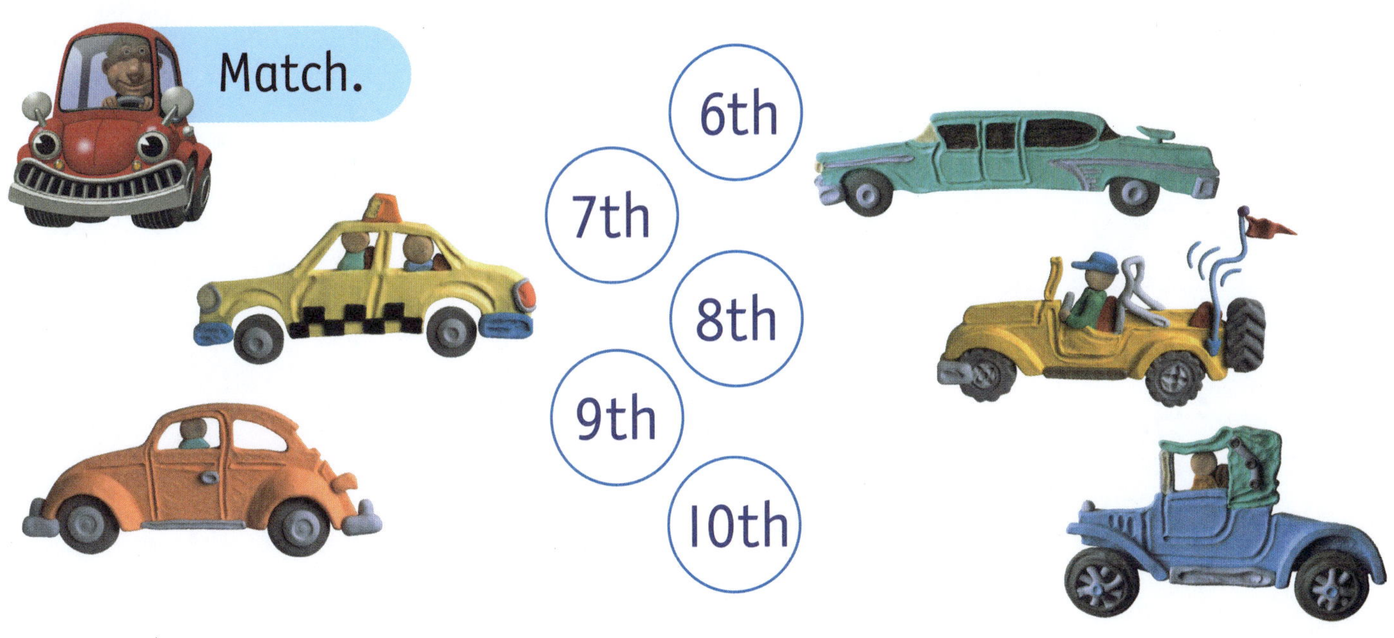

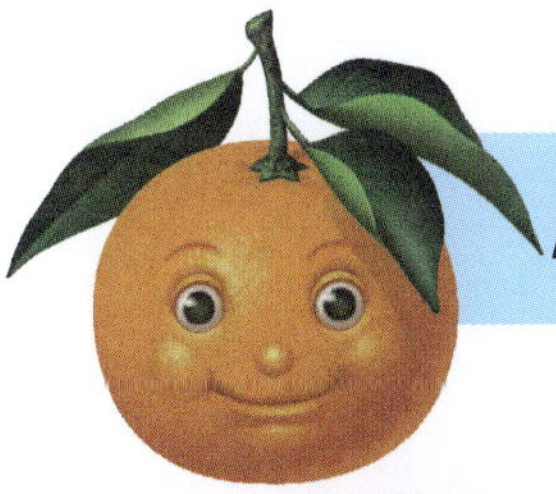

Award prizes for 1st, 2nd, 3rd and 4th.

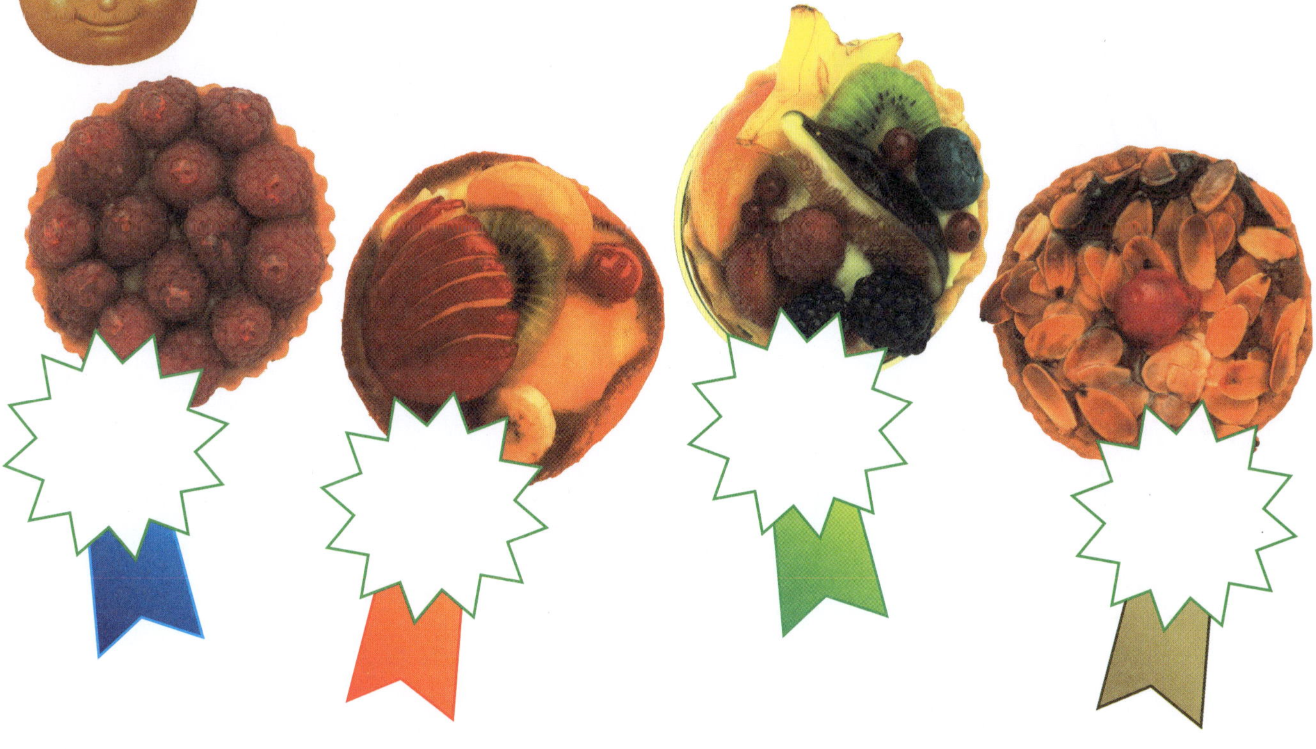

# Number names to thirty

| | |
|---|---|
| twenty-one | 21 |
| twenty-two | 22 |
| twenty-three | 23 |
| twenty-four | 24 |
| twenty-five | 25 |
| twenty-six | 26 |
| twenty-seven | 27 |
| twenty-eight | 28 |
| twenty-nine | 29 |
| thirty | 30 |

| | |
|---|---|
| 26 | twenty-eight |
| 28 | twenty |
| 20 | twenty-six |
| 27 | twenty-three |
| 23 | twenty-seven |

Write the numbers.

twenty-two

twenty-nine

twenty-five

thirty



**Number • AC9MFN01** name, represent and order numbers including zero to at least 20, using physical and virtual materials and numerals

# Counting forwards and backwards

Write the missing numbers.

| | | | | |
|---|---|---|---|---|
| 16 | | 18 | 19 | |
| 21 | | 23 | 24 | 25 |
| | 27 | 28 | | 30 |

| | | | |
|---|---|---|---|
| 22 | 24 | 28 | 30 |
| 23 | 23 | | |
| | 22 | 26 | |
| | | | |
| | | | 26 |

# Tens and ones

How many?

Draw a number.



**Number • AC9MFN01** name, represent and order numbers including zero to at least 20, using physical and virtual materials and numerals

# Using a number line

Write the missing numbers.

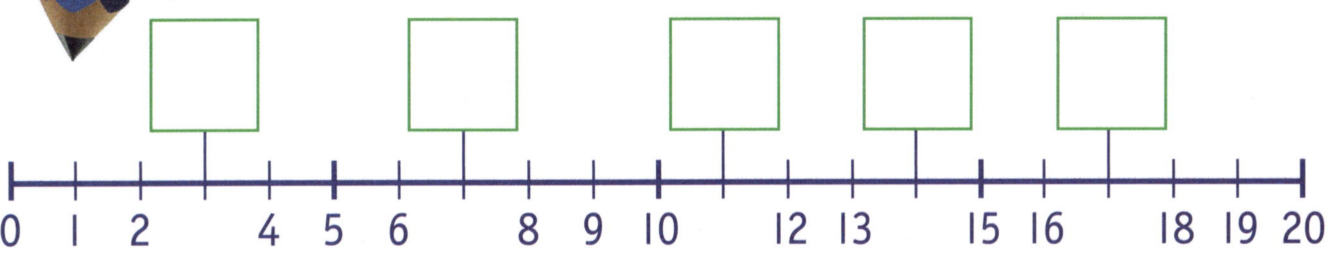


Match.

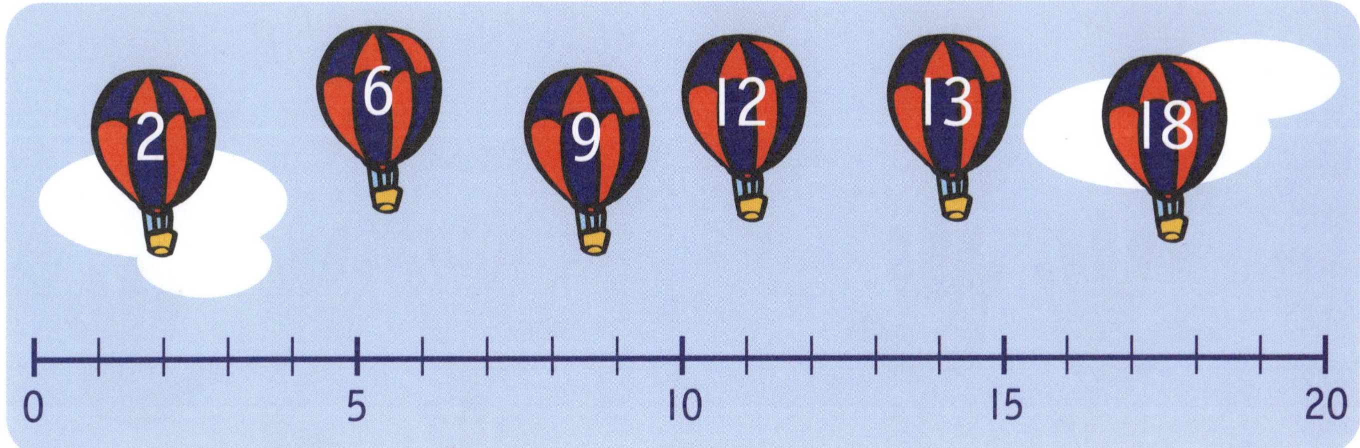


Write the numbers.

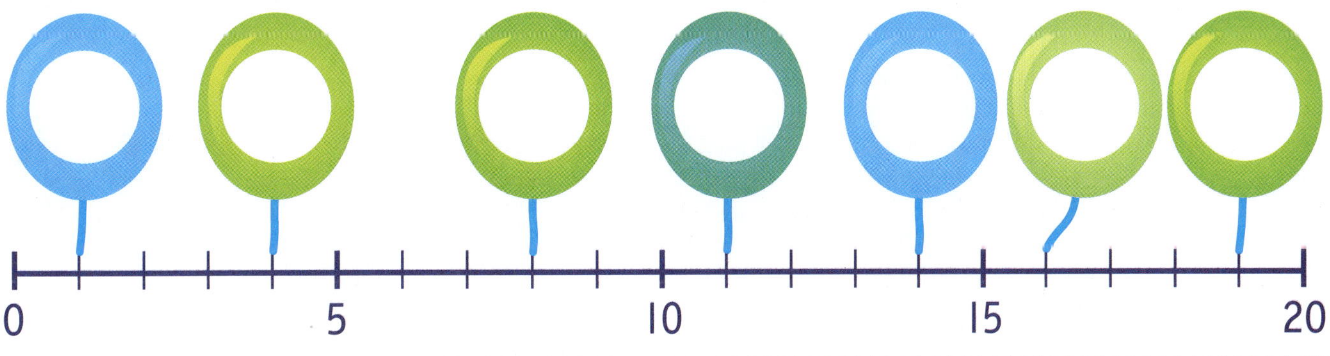


**Challenge!** Estimate the numbers.

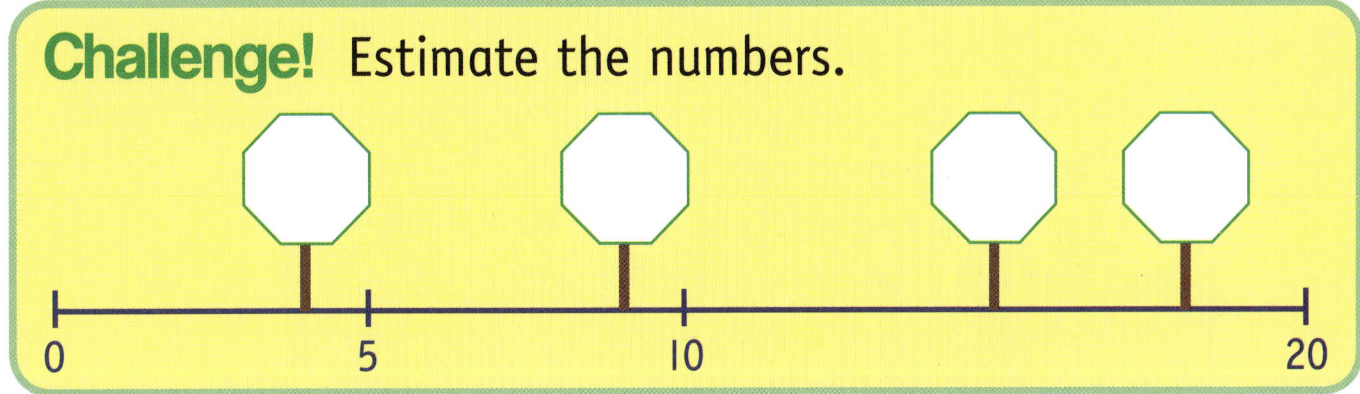

# Counting to thirty

1 2 3 4 5 6 7 8 9 **10** 11 12 13 14 15 16 17 18 19 **20** 21 22 23 24 25 26 27 28 29 **30**

How many fingers?

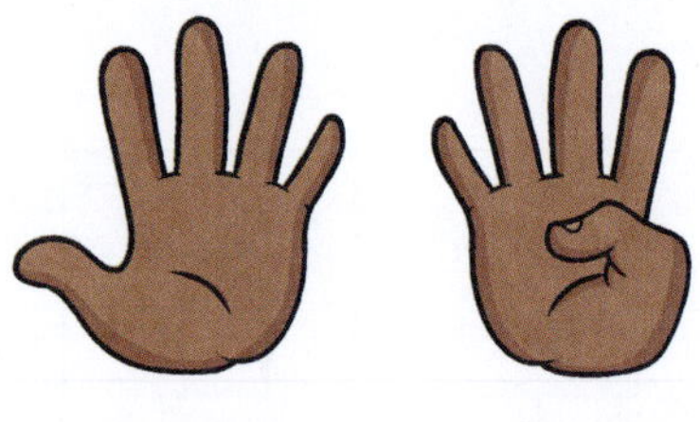

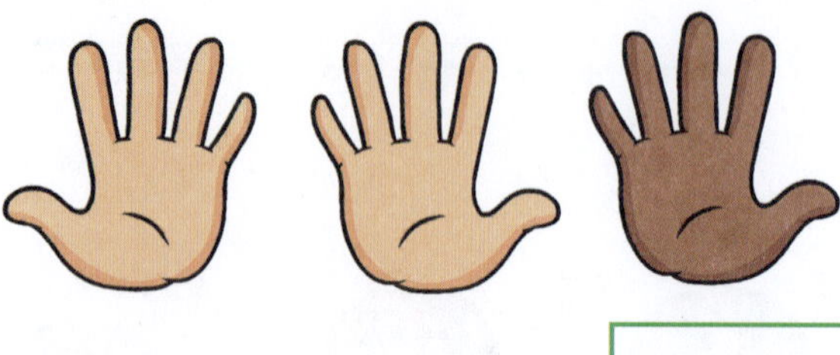

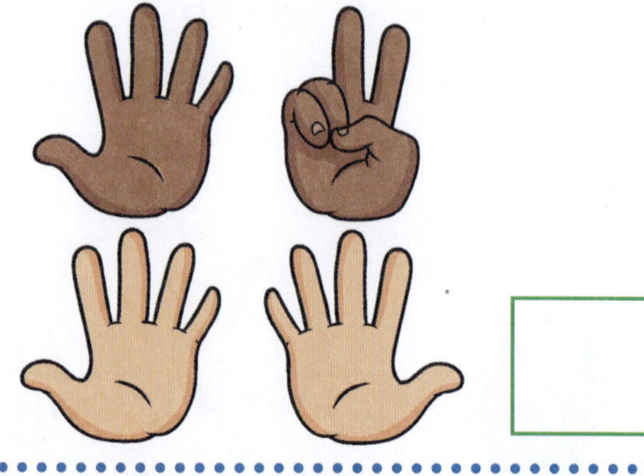

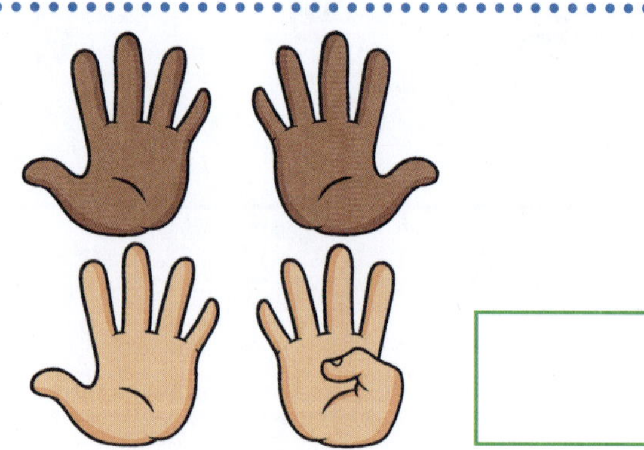

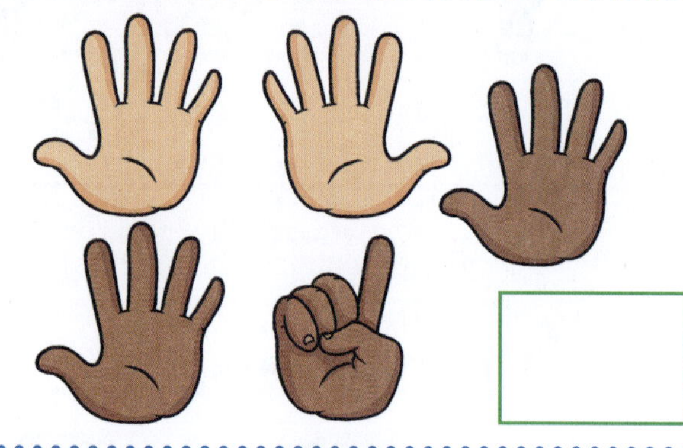

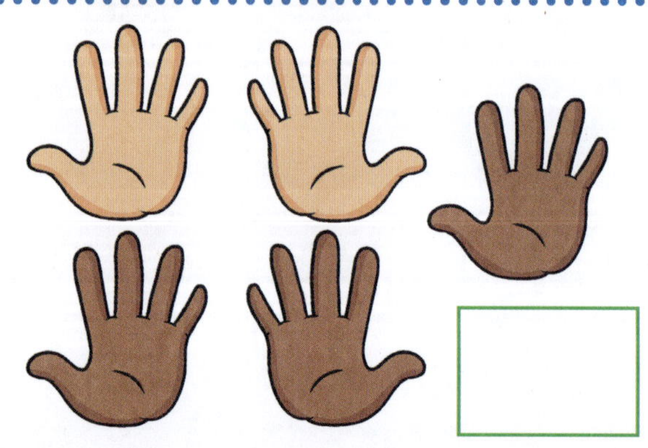

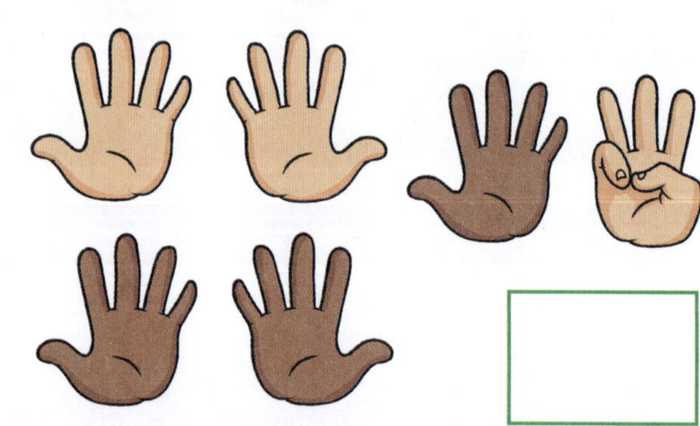

## Mastery Checklist

I can:

- ☐ use the ordinal names to tenth.
- ☐ show numbers using objects, number words and numerals.
- ☐ count forwards to 30 and backwards from 30.
- ☐ read numerals to 30, including zero.



**Number** • **AC9MFN01** name, represent and order numbers to at least 20 • **AC9MFN02** recognise the number of objects within a collection using subitising

# Number Problems

Use the number line to solve the problems.

1 Lin has 15 balls. May has 1 more than Lin.
Nick has 1 less than Lin.
How many balls do May and Nick have?

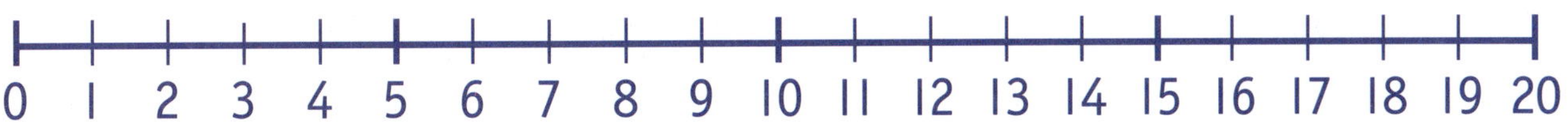


May ______ balls    Nick ______ balls

2 Amy has 1 more ring than Ben. Cam has 1 less ring than Amy. Ben has 12 rings.
How many rings do Amy and Cam have?

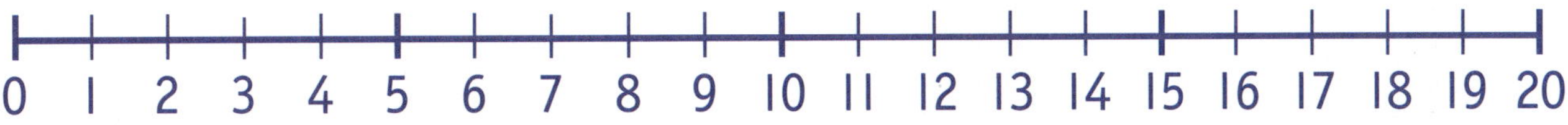


Amy ______ rings    Cam ______ rings

I can solve problems by:

☐ identifying the number after or before a number. ☐ using a number line.

# Digital and analogue time

## Saturday

☐ o'clock

☐ o'clock

☐ o'clock

☐ o'clock

☐ o'clock

☐ o'clock

# Problem solving

## Your day

Draw and write about your Saturday.

☐ o'clock

☐ o'clock

☐ o'clock

☐ o'clock

☐ o'clock

☐ o'clock

I can solve a problem by:

☐ putting events in time order. ☐ drawing a picture.

# Volume

Circle the one that takes up the most space.

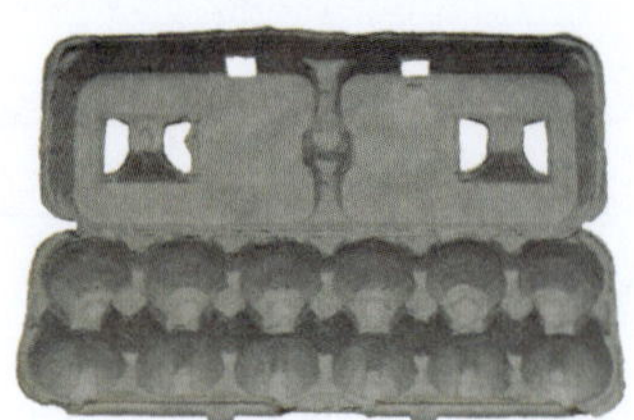

Draw something that takes up less space.

# Measuring capacity

measure **capacity** in cups

## How many [cup] fill each one?

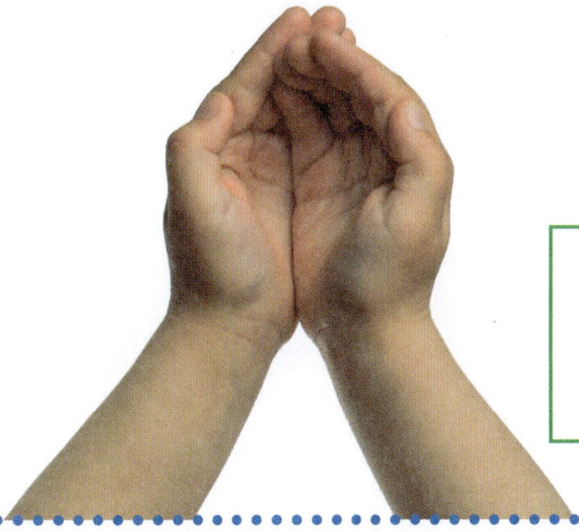

## Draw what happens next.

## Mastery Checklist

I can:
- ☐ read analogue and digital clocks to the hour using the term 'o'clock'.
- ☐ put events in time order.
- ☐ identify volume as the amount of space an object takes up.
- ☐ fill and empty containers.

# Comparing groups

6 

4 

 How many more?  

 How many more?  

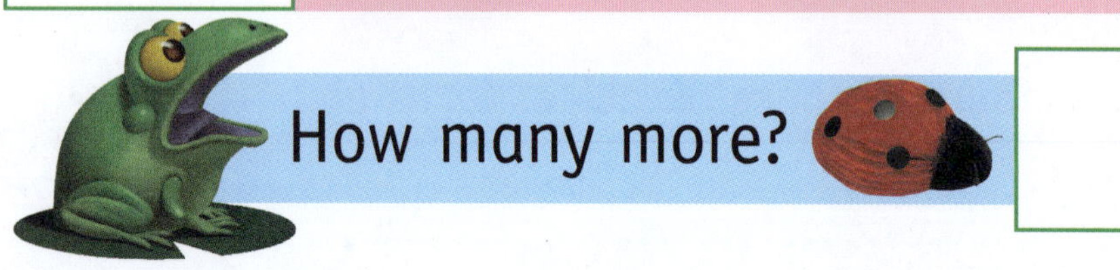 How many more?

 **Number** • **AC9MFN03** quantify and compare collections to at least 20 • **AC9MFN05** represent practical situations involving addition, subtraction and quantification

# Shopping with dollar coins

Cross out the coins to buy.

How much left?

$2

$1 $1 $1 $1 $1
$1 $1 $1 $1 $1

$5

$1 $1 $1 $1 $1
$1 $1 $1 $1 $1

$6

$1 $1 $1 $1 $1
$1 $1 $1 $1 $1

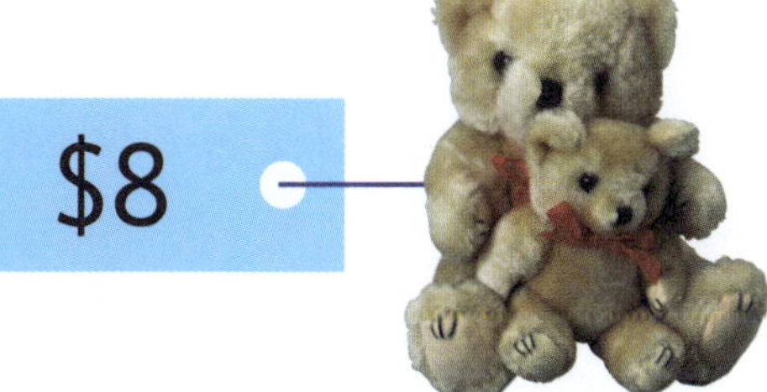

$8

$1 $1 $1 $1 $1
$1 $1 $1 $1 $1

**Challenge!** Each domino should have 10 dots.
Draw the missing dots.

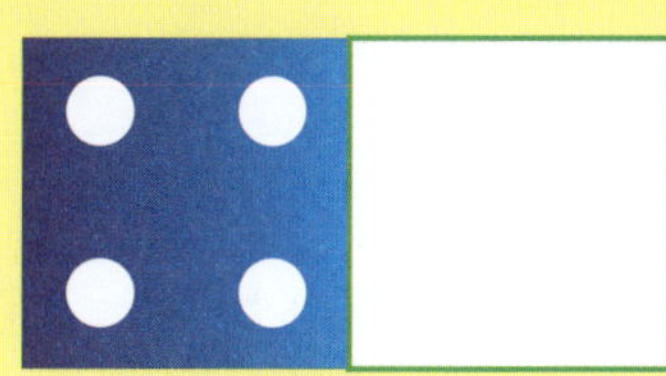

# Counting back

Count back 1.

This sign means take away.

$6 - 1 = \square$

1 2 3 4 5 6 7 8 9 10

$3 - 1 = \square$

1 2 3 4 5 6 7 8 9 10

$9 - 1 = \square$

1 2 3 4 5 6 7 8 9 10

$7 - 1 = \square$

Count back 2.

1 2 3 4 5 6 7 8 9 10

$8 - 2 = \square$

1 2 3 4 5 6 7 8 9 10

$5 - 2 = \square$

1 2 3 4 5 6 7 8 9 10

$10 - 2 = \square$

1 2 3 4 5 6 7 8 9 10

$9 - 2 = \square$

# Subtraction

**– means take away.**

4 - 3 = ☐

5 - 2 = ☐

7 - 2 = ☐

6 - 3 = ☐

5 - ☐ = ☐

7 - ☐ = ☐

8 - ☐ = ☐

10 - ☐ = ☐

## Challenge!

7 cats. 2 run away. 2 hide.

How many left? ☐

## Mastery Checklist

I can:

- ☐ compare two groups of objects to find how many more.
- ☐ count by ones to find the difference.
- ☐ take away part of a group of objects to show subtraction.
- ☐ use diagrams to help with separating quantities.

# Block it up

Investigation 4

Make these shapes out of blocks.
How many blocks in each shape?

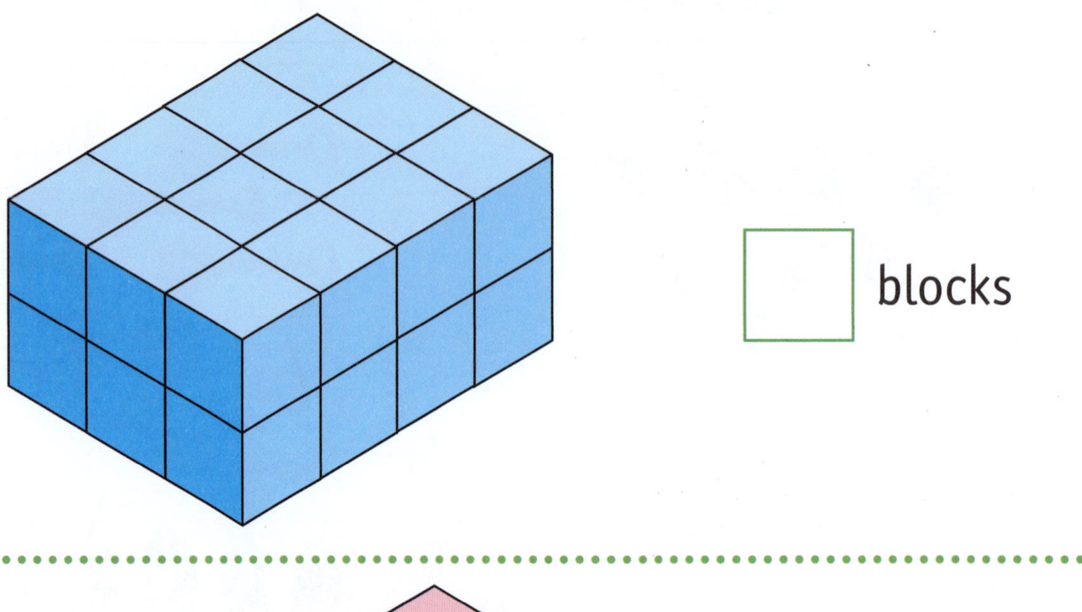

☐ blocks

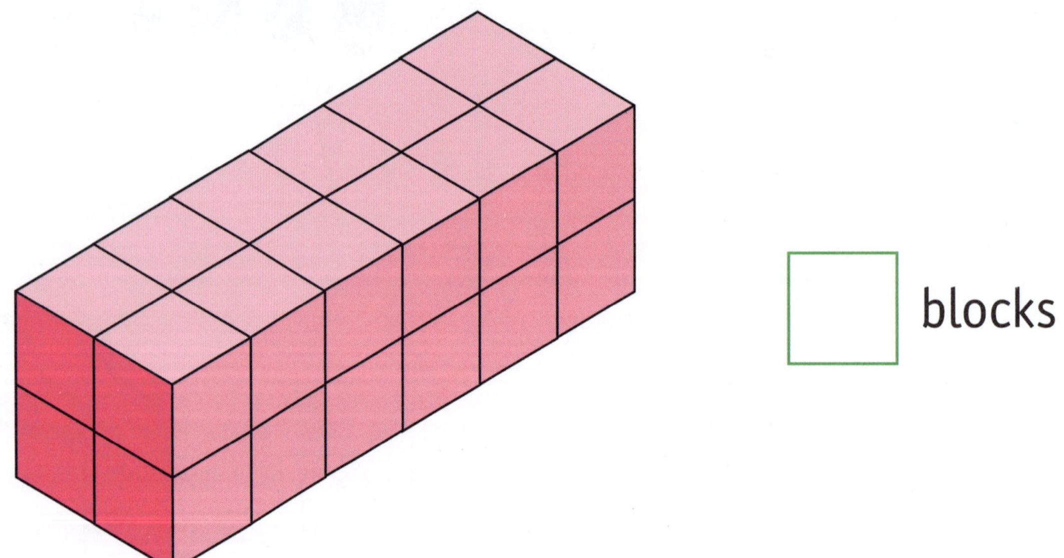

☐ blocks

Complete the sentence:

more    less    the same    as    than

The first shape has __________ blocks __________ the second shape.

# Block it up

Investigation 4

Make the first shape using the blocks from the second shape. Draw it here:

Make the second shape using the blocks from the first shape. Draw it here:

To do this, I needed to:

- [ ] make a variety of 3D models.
- [ ] stack and pack blocks into defined spaces.
- [ ] compare the volumes of two objects made from blocks.
- [ ] deconstruct one object and use its parts to make the other.
- [ ] use comparative language to describe volume.

I enjoyed this task!

☆☆☆☆☆

# Revision

**1** How many fingers? ☐

**2** What colour shirt is:

2nd? ______________

5th? ______________

6th? ______________

How many balloons are there?

less than 10 ☐ less than 20 ☐ more than 20 ☐

**3** Write the missing days.

| Sunday |
| --- |
| |
| Tuesday |

| Wednesday |
| --- |
| Thursday |
| |
| Saturday |

# Revision

**4** Colour.

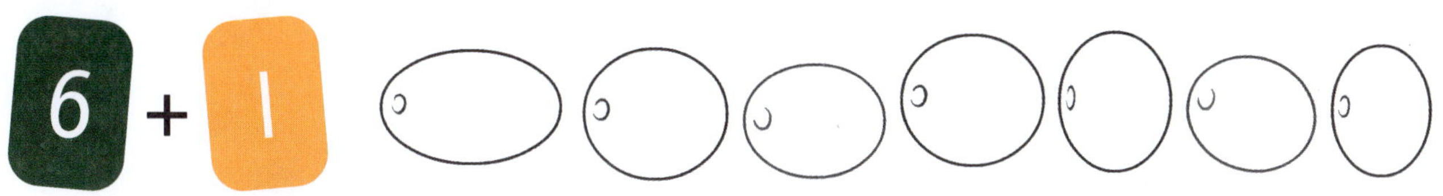

3 + 4

**5**

$2 + 5 = \square$ $\quad$ $1 + 6 = \square$

$7 + 0 = \square$ $\quad$ $4 + 3 = \square$

**6** Use three numbers.

$\square + \square + \square = 7$

# Sharing

Share.

How many each? ☐

How many each? ☐

# Sharing

Share.

How many each?

How many each?

# Equal shares

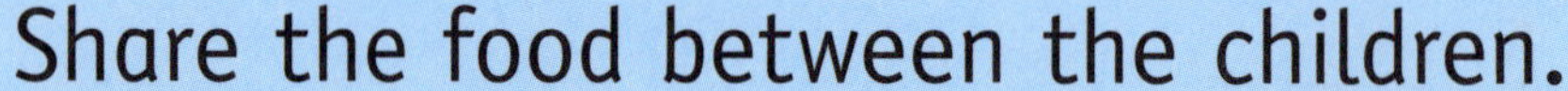

Share the food between the children.

Give each child a knife and fork.



**Number • AC9MFN06** represent practical situations involving equal sharing and grouping with physical and virtual materials and use counting or subitising strategies

# Problem solving

## Cars

20 children want to go to the park. There are 5 cars.

Each car must take the same number of children.

How many children go in each car? ________

I can solve a problem by:

☐ sharing a group of objects into smaller groups. ☐ drawing a picture.

# Comparing mass by hefting

Mass

compare **weight** by hefting

Use some of these.

**Mass is how heavy or light.**

Draw.

is heavier than

is heavier than

is heavier than

is heavier than

# Using an equal arm balance

Draw something

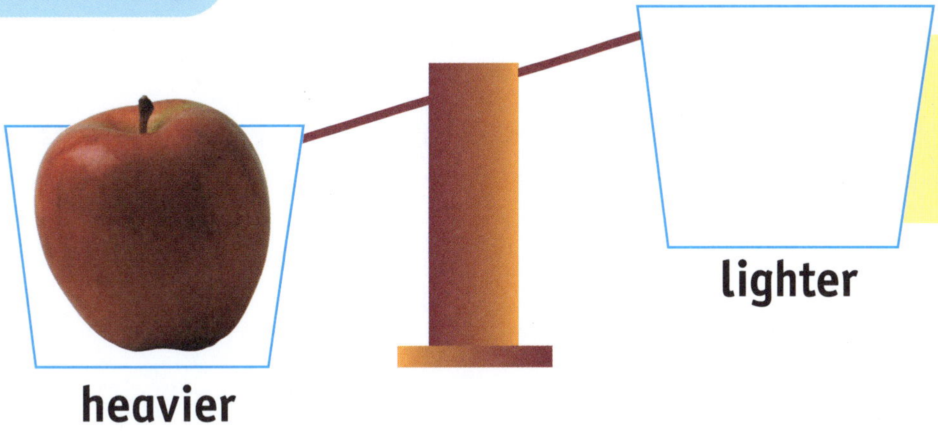

lighter than an apple.

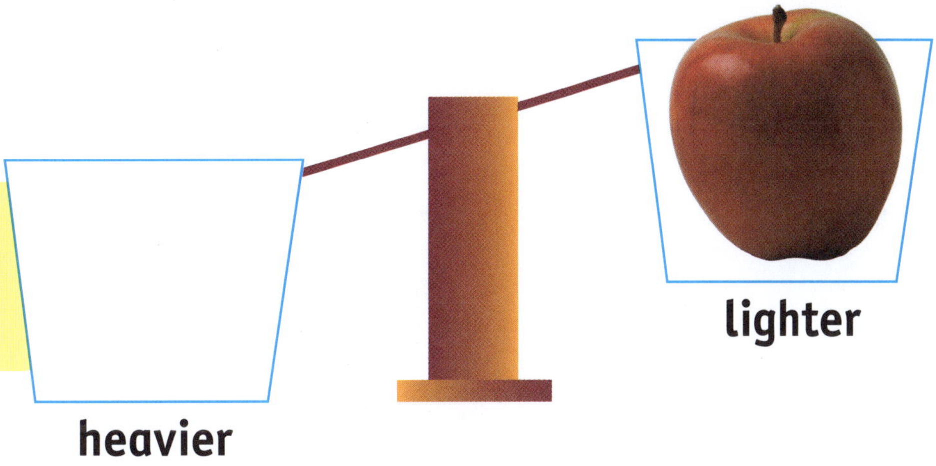

heavier

lighter

heavier than an apple.

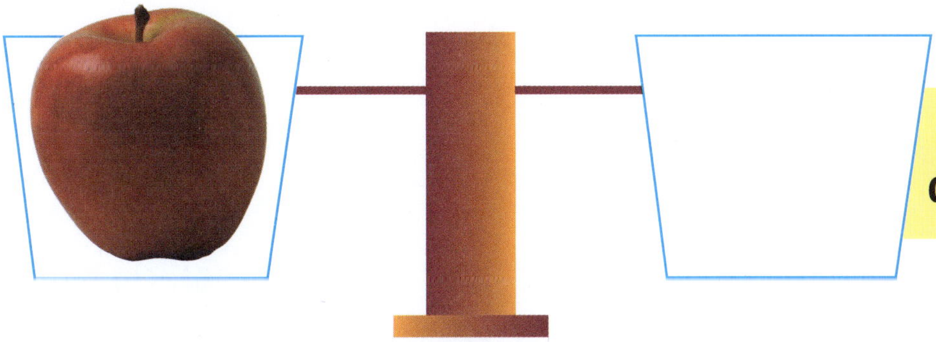

heavier

lighter

same as an apple.

Circle the lightest object on the page.

## Mastery Checklist

I can:
- [ ] share a group of objects into smaller groups.
- [ ] label the number of objects in a group.
- [ ] compare two masses by hefting.
- [ ] predict which object would be heavier, lighter or about the same.

# Sorting 3D objects

**Colour** the flat surfaces.

**Colour** the curved surfaces.

Circle the pointy corners.



**Space • AC9MFSP01** sort, name and create familiar shapes; recognise and describe familiar shapes within objects in the environment, giving reasons

# 3D objects

Use colours to match.

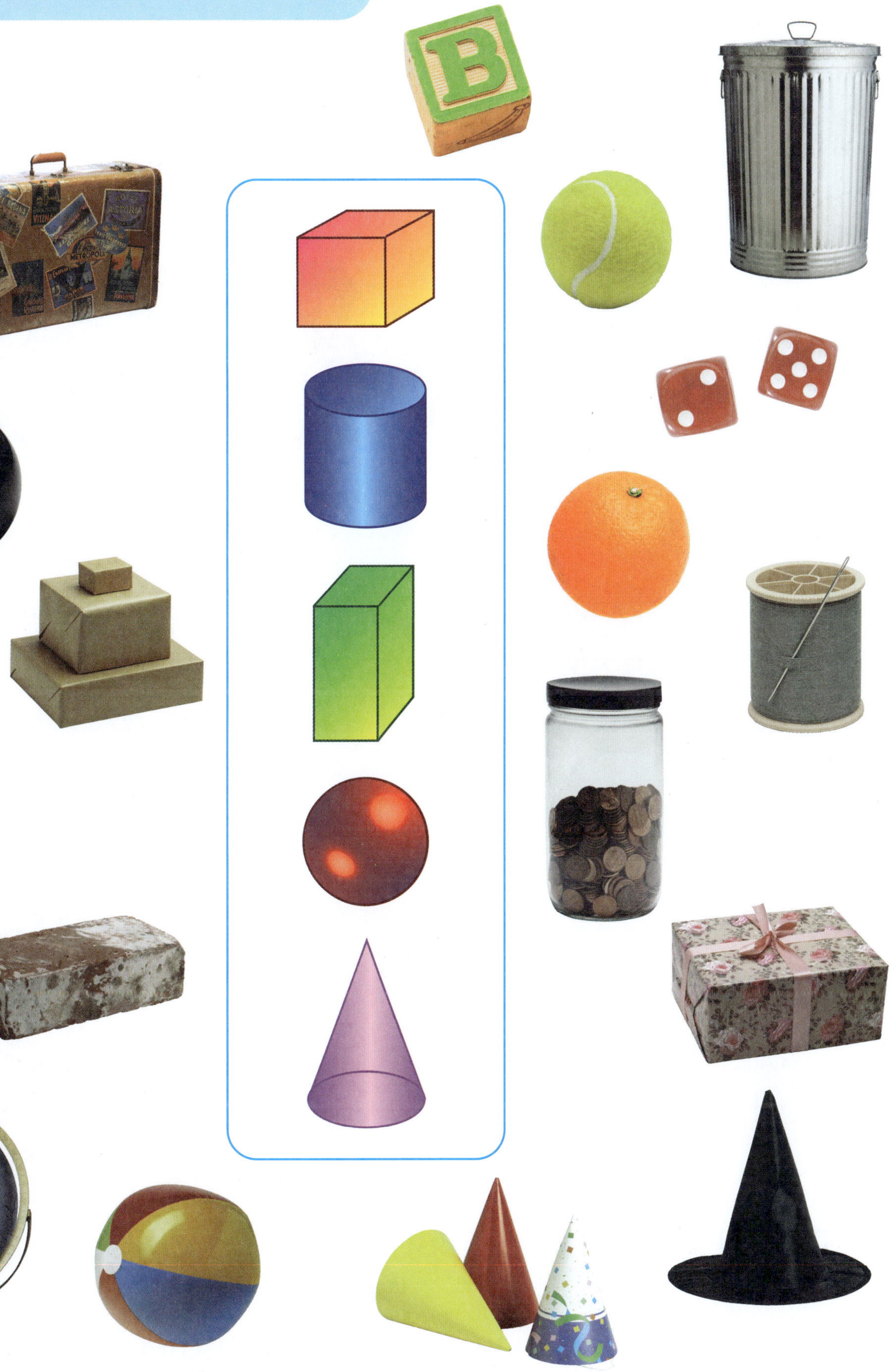

# Reading a picture graph

## Shirts or jumpers?

Shirts

Jumpers

### How many?

girls 

boys 

### How many children have:

black hair? 

brown hair? 

blonde hair? 

red hair? 

How many children altogether? 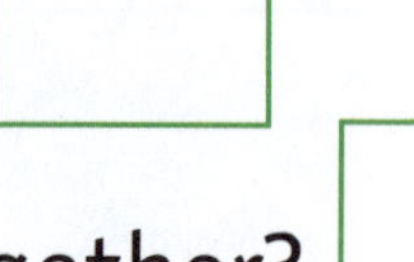

# Make a picture graph

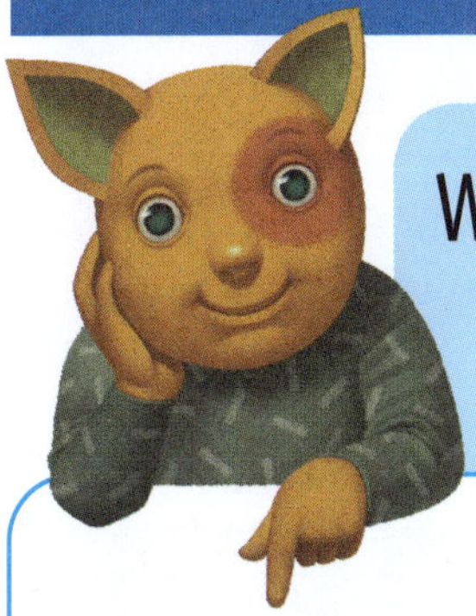

What colour are your eyes?

Count the eye colours in your class.

Colour a box for each person.

| | | | | | | |
|---|---|---|---|---|---|---|
| blue eyes | | | | | | |
| | | | | | | |
| brown eyes | | | | | | |
| | | | | | | |
| green eyes | | | | | | |
| | | | | | | |

How many? ..........

What is the most common eye colour?

# Estimation to 20

Estimate how many stars. Circle your guess.

**Estimate**
**Make a close guess.**

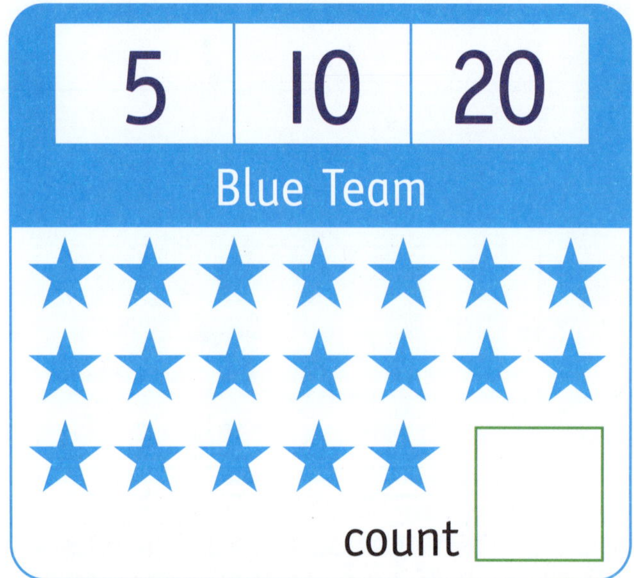

**Challenge!**

Look at each star chart.
How many more to make 20?

## Mastery Checklist

I can:
- ☐ sort objects and identify how I sorted them.
- ☐ describe the features of familiar objects.
- ☐ answer questions about data collected.
- ☐ collect data and form a data display.

**Number • AC9MFN01** name, represent and order numbers including zero to at least 20, using physical and virtual materials and numerals

# Revision • Term 4

1 How many?

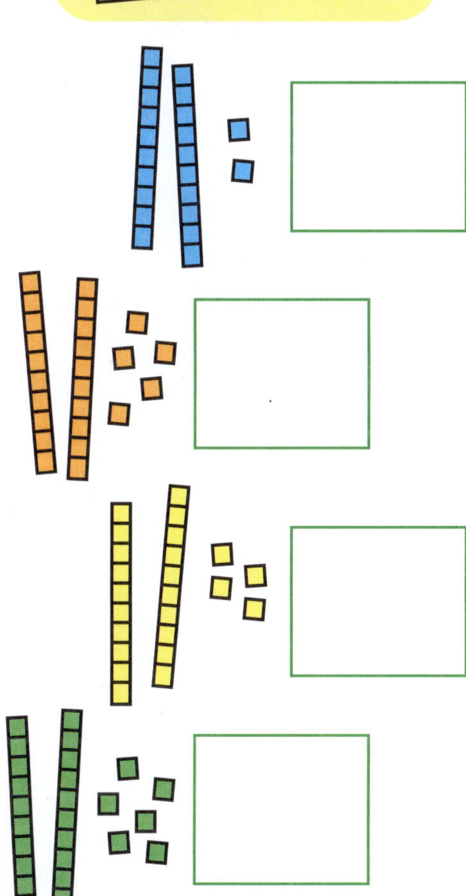


2 Write the missing numbers.

25

29

30

28

3 Colour one half of each shape.

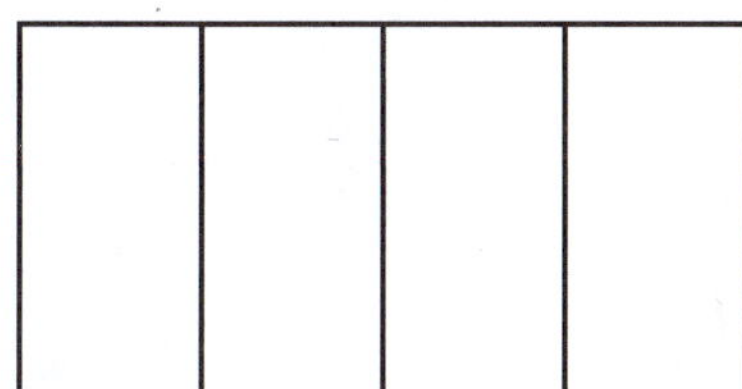

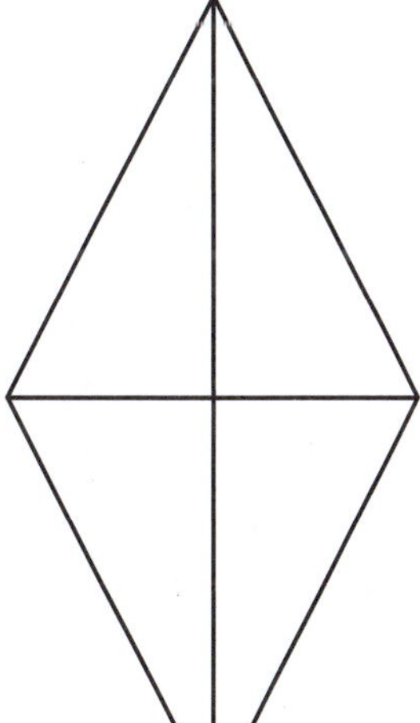

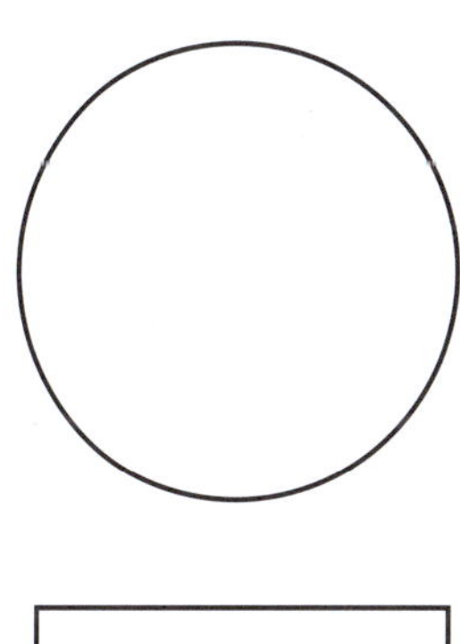

# Revision • Term 4

**4** Circle the coins to buy.

**5** What time is it?

**6** How many groups of two?